MW01258107

THE
LAUREL
BOOK

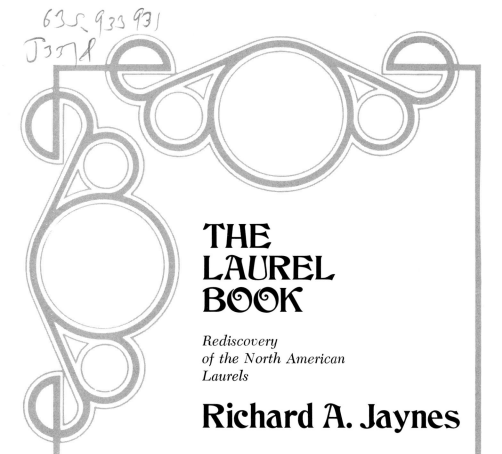

THE LAUREL BOOK

Rediscovery of the North American Laurels

Richard A. Jaynes

HAFNER PRESS
A Division of Macmillan Publishing Co., Inc.
NEW YORK
Collier Macmillan Publishers
LONDON

Hafner Press
A Division of Macmillan Publishing Co., Inc.
866 Third Avenue, New York, N.Y. 10022

Collier Macmillan Canada, Ltd.

Library of Congress Catalog Card Number: 75-20015

Library of Congress Cataloging in Publication Data

Jaynes, Richard A
    The laurel book.

    Bibliography: p.
    Includes index.
    1. Kalmia. 2. Mountain laurel. 3. Botany--
North America. I. Title.
SB413.K3J39   635.9'33'931   75-20015
ISBN 0-02-847180-6

Printed in the United States of America

printing number

1 2 3 4 5 6 7 8 9 10

Contents

Preface

The mountain laurel of the American states (Kalmia latifolia) is one of those plants which, if of recent introduction, would be eagerly sought after; but having been an inhabitant of our gardens for nearly a century and a half, it receives but little attention. (Alpha—pen name for anonymous author—1882)

Mountain laurel, the favorite garden laurel, has been admired and cultivated since the discovery of America. It is the state flower of both Connecticut and Pennsylvania and is native to the twenty-three states from Louisiana to Ohio and east to the Atlantic. It is grown extensively in southeastern Canada and in the northwestern United States. All seven laurel species are indigenous to North America, and between the western laurel and the southern coastal species at least one variety will thrive in any garden in the continental United States. Yet, from an experimentalist's point of view, laurel has been completely neglected.

Prior to 1961, when the Connecticut Agricultural Experiment Station began a breeding and genetic study of all the *Kalmia* species, no one had successfully bred laurel. Indeed, hardly anyone had tried. The neglect of laurel is even more puzzling when one considers that the closely related rhododendrons have been successfully hybridized in large numbers for more than 150 years. Why laurel has been neglected is unknown. Perhaps it was feared the obstacles would be great and the rewards small.

But today renewed interest in all native American plants and in their garden value has led to a reawakening to the possibilities of the laurels. In this book we attempt to show that the obstacles to cultivation of the laurels are not many and that the rewards are indeed great. So here for the first time is the record of the laurel's history, botany, taxonomy, genetics, culture, and propagation—a record which stresses the genetic variation and rich diversity among the plants in the laurel genus. Lines of future research and development are sketched, and the cultivars (varieties) worthy of propagation are identified. Like all books of this nature, information on the "best cultivars" and pest control chemicals will become outdated, but we hope that this book will provide a basic reference of immediate and lasting value to the gardener, the student, the horticulturist, and the nurseryman.

We invite you to rediscover the long-neglected laurels, a favorite and familiar American plant. But we warn you that you may experience some frustration, for mountain laurel selections are at present difficult to root and slow growing; hence, named cultivars are not readily available. The situation is, however, improving, and growers with the patience to work with woody plants, which often may take more than five years from seed to flower, will learn to enjoy the excitement and discovery that the waiting itself brings: Every day and every season the plants change, and watching them grow, develop, and mature is its own reward. Add to this the challenge of developing improved cultural methods, and you have added another dimension to the breeding of new varieties. Our first mountain laurel seedlings took nearly eight years to flower. With the improved techniques described in this book, we now routinely obtain flowers in the fifth year, and we can realistically predict a day when most of our plants will bloom in their fourth year.

After your first group of seedlings mature and flower, you will be trapped, and in your mind, if not in your garden, a procession of new flowering types will bloom. So you had better get started. . . .

Richard A. Jaynes
December 1974

Acknowledgments

Study and experimentation are never done entirely independently, nor are they ever entirely self-motivated. At the Connecticut Agricultural Experiment Station an atmosphere conducive to independent research was engendered by my department head and graduate school adviser, the late Donald F. Jones, and has been invaluable to me in my work. My interest in laurel crystallized in 1960 and was nurtured under the stimulating guidance of Harry T. Stinson, Jr., successor to Dr. Jones. Other colleagues at the Connecticut station, former and present, to whom I am indebted include John F. Ahrens, Carl D. Clayberg, Peter R. Day, Dennis Dunbar, William L. George, Jr., Gary Heickel, Bruce Minor, George Stephens, and Gerald Walton. Several college students found the research a challenging summer endeavor. I am particularly indebted to Rita Sorensen Leonard, Mark Neuffer, and Richard Wetzler for their cheerful, valuable assistance. Many of the drawings are

by Mrs. Leonard. John E. Ebinger's
contribution goes well beyond the two
chapters he wrote, "Laurels in the Wild"
and "Toxicity of Laurel Foliage." His
tireless efforts in completing the taxonomic
study of the genus are notable, and I am
indebted to him for the insights gained
in our many lively debates and discussions
on *Kalmia*. My wife and children soon
found that my interests in laurel were not
limited to the confines of the experiment
station. They gave support and
understanding as seedlings, grafts, and
cuttings took over our greenhouse and
grounds.

It is impossible to list all the gardeners,
nurserymen, horticulturists, and botanists
in this country and Europe who have
contributed materials and ideas. Their
cooperation and enthusiasm have been an
inspiration to me and an indication of
the wide interest in these plants. With
pleasure I cite the three generations of
Mezitts of Weston Nurseries, Hopkinton,
Massachusetts, who, in my many visits,
literally made available any laurel that
caught my eye. Finally, the diligent
typing of Evelyn Breuler and the dedicated
assistance of Edward Quigley and his
staff at Hafner are acknowledged.

Most of the photographs were taken
by the author. Illustrative material is
credited to the Connecticut Agricultural
Experiment Station unless otherwise noted.

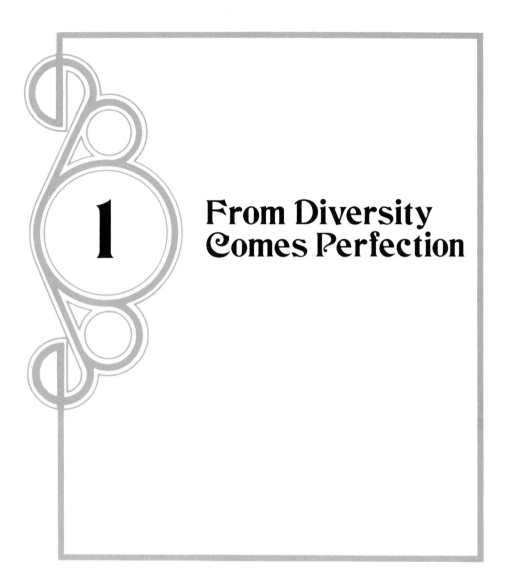

1

From Diversity Comes Perfection

"Wouldn't you like to have been the genetist who developed laurel?" Donald F. Jones, famous for his work in genetics and the development of hybrid corn, once asked this question of a colleague. Here was the perfect shrub—flowering, evergreen, hardy. But if it were "perfect," there would be no need for the experimenter. As we shall see, it is neither uniform nor perfect. Mountain laurel and its close relatives exhibit wide variation and give the grower opportunity for selection and manipulation.

A common misconception, even among those familiar with the plant, is that only a single good plant or clone exists of the unusual kinds of mountain laurel; that is to say, one red-bud, one deep pink, or one miniature. This book should dispel that misconception. The characteristics that make these forms unique are under the control of one or several genes. The number of plants of any one form is limited only by the number of seedlings of the right parentage that we can grow. While each seedling may be slightly different from every other one, it will be recognizable as a particular form as long as it carries the right determinant genes. The more seedlings that are raised to flowering age, the better our chance of selecting individuals which surpass existing clonal selections.

By growing varieties of laurel seedlings, we are merely doing— in a convenient way—something that nature does on its own every year. Obviously, nature's way of sowing on bare mineral soil in a shaded or protected spot is a successful, if much slower, means to the same end. The special way we treat the plants is designed to speed up the process and make it more efficient and selective.

An advantage of growing large populations of selected seedlings is that we can improve other characteristics along with the one of particular interest. For example, red-budded mountain laurel tends to have fewer, smaller, and more twisted leaves than the pink or white selections, and it flowers a few days later. With additional breeding and selection, red-budded seedlings with dense foliage and broad, flat leaves can be developed. Weston Nurseries has selected, and propagated by grafting, a low-growing, densely branched red-bud. If it can be propagated from cuttings, it will become a named cultivar. Keep in mind, in making your own experiments, that in selecting for one trait it is important that other good plant characteristics are not neglected or weakened.

Our search for better laurel has been filled with its own excitements, adventures, and rewards. To sample the natural variations of the *Kalmia*, we canvassed botanical gardens, nurserymen, and home gardeners, asking about unusual and distinctive kinds. Slowly we began to accumulate selections and information on the limits of variation.

One of my first memorable encounters was with a man who managed a whole mountainside of laurel which was open to the public during the nearby town's annual June laurel festival. I asked him if he had ever noticed any plants with unusual flowers or foliage. Of course he had, but he solemnly assured me that in spite of these variations, all mountain laurel was really the same. Any differences, he said, were due to different exposures and varying amounts of minerals, such as copper and iron, in the soil. Fortunately, in our work this interesting theory turns out to be false.

Having worked with woody plants before, we anticipated the need for patience. We did not anticipate that in several cases the real test would be in actually obtaining the material in the first place. Some people, perhaps with good reason, are highly reluctant to share the unusual plant they have. For example, learning of a unique mountain laurel clone in 1963, I wrote for a few scions. The ensuing correspondence makes quite a file, and it was not until I had exchanged—over a decade!—numerous letters about the plant with three different persons, that cuttings were finally obtained. Happily, such stories are the exception and not the rule.

No amount of persistence, however, has succeeded in my obtaining live material from two mountain laurels with atypical foliage growing in the southern Appalachians. Herbarium (pressed) specimens have been made of the plants, but the only person who allegedly knows of their location simply does not answer letters.

Failure to obtain a plant is not the only frustration facing the plant breeder. Sometimes the people cooperate and the plants don't. Ralph Smith found a sectored mountain laurel in New York, but the first few scions he sent me failed to take upon grafting. When I requested more material for another try two years later, it was too late. The plant had died. This was a hard-earned lesson on the need to propagate immediately any unusual, potentially valuable plants to ensure their preservation.

Plain luck also plays its part in acquiring unusual plants. Robert Bird of the Bristol Nursery in Bristol, Connecticut, tells this amusing story about a fabulous broad-banded laurel of theirs. In the fall they did some landscaping for a woman in town. When the laurel plantings began to flower the following June, she called them to complain that the flowers in one of the plants were abnormal. A nurseryman was sent to examine the plant. Within minutes of his arrival he obligingly replaced it with a "normal" one. The abnormal, broad-banded one, among the most attractive ever found, is now proudly displayed in front of the Bristol Nursery.

In addition to seeking unusual laurels, we searched for representative seeds or seedlings of the different species from numerous locations within their native ranges. On one trip to Peaked Hill Pond, near Thornton, New Hampshire, I arrived late in the day and camped, in the loosest sense of the word, in nearby White Mountain National Forest. It was one of the worst nights I've ever spent: I had only a sleeping bag, no tent, and no netting; and the tiny no-see'ems greeted me in swarms. To sleep with my head in the bag meant suffocation; to sleep with my head out meant torture. So shortly after 3 A.M., I gave up and went for a walk in the moonlight. At dawn I drove to Thornton and started the 2½ mile trek from the road into the laurel stand. By sunup I reached it, collected a few small plants, seeds, flowers, and cuttings, and by 7:30 I was back at the local restaurant for breakfast.

The sun was well up by 9 when I got back to the laurels to take pictures. It was truly an idyllic setting with beaver pond, laurel in bloom, a sugar bush nearby, wildflowers beneath the trees, and bird songs. This was worth one night with no-see-'ems.

To my disappointment a few years later I learned that this northern strain of mountain laurel—which we assumed would be very hardy—was, in fact, very weak. Compared with every other source tested, it did poorly in either sun or shade. The only explanation is that the laurel at Peaked Hill Pond is an isolated population and may have suffered from inbreeding depression.

To collect laurel specimens along Connecticut state highways and on state lands, I obtained a special permit from the state capital. But, because of the state law which forbids collecting laurel and the public stigma attached to it, I felt self-conscious digging up plants along the roads in full view of passersby. But I stuck to it and one summer I searched for the pinkest and the whitest laurel in the state. My assistant, in response to my guilt feelings, had developed the ability to dig and load a 3-foot plant in less than a minute. As we approached a previously spotted plant, he would hop out of the truck as we rolled to a stop, shovel in hand. By the time I could turn the truck around, he would be waiting to put the plant aboard. The only plants I remember not surviving this snatching technique were those that came out of deep shade and ones which were not pruned heavily on transplanting.

Now that I am known as a laurel "fanatic," news of striking and remarkable plants sometimes comes to me out of the blue. For example, I learned of the native stand of mountain laurel which includes 'Goodrich' and other banded laurels through Henry Fuller of the American Rock Garden Society. He had not seen the plants himself, but he had heard that there were some purple-flowered mountain laurel near Willimantic, Connecticut. Fuller was skeptical, because he said the report had come from an economics professor and not a biologist. I wrote the professor's friend who had first-hand knowledge of the laurel, fully expecting to find it was nothing more than a native stand of sheep laurel. But to my surprise the letter to John Goodrich was answered immediately, and his answer contained colored slides of the unusual banded flowers. On a visit to the native stand in June, I discovered at least twenty of the banded plants. The best has been used in some recent crosses, and the most heavily pigmented one has been named 'Goodrich' as a tribute to the man who discovered it.

News of other laurels has come to me from farther away. One day I received a letter from Marjorie and Hollis Rogers of Greensboro, North Carolina. They had enclosed a slide of a completely unknown mountain laurel. Here was a new flower type of the genus, found in the wild more than 800 miles away. Through the Rogers' wonderful cooperation, within weeks we had cuttings for grafts, pollen for crosses, and seeds for planting. The result is a newly named cultivar, 'Shooting Star.'

Closer to home, Dan Cappel, a high school biology teacher from Wilton, Connecticut, discovered a plant like 'Shooting Star' that blooms about two weeks later than normal mountain laurel. Unfortunately, because it has a split style and appears to be pollen- and seed-sterile, we may not be able to use it for crosses. Further observation of the original, the grafts, and the rooted cuttings will determine its ultimate ornamental value.

These recent discoveries of new laurel variants convince me that there are many other variations to be found, and, as each distinct form is discovered, breeding possibilities will increase.

It would take a crystal ball to predict how these selections of mountain laurel will be propagated in the future. But some speculation is in order. Some will definitely continue to be grown from seed, and, if the seed parentage is carefully controlled, the seedlings will be all the more valuable. If named selections are to receive wide distribution, propagation from cuttings will be essential. The selection of easy-to-root clones, plus improved techniques, will permit greater success with cutting propagation. Grafting will fill the need for immediate propagation of one-of-a-kind plants, particularly those which are difficult to root and/or not readily obtained from seed.

Since propagation and culture are among the chief concerns of the nurseryman, only those plants which he can propagate and grow economically will be available for the home gardener.

So more research is needed on propagating and growing laurel to flowering size. The generally poor success in rooting cuttings and the generally long period from seed to flowering may discourage some commercial plant propagators, and even plant hobbyists, but I do predict that future gains will reward present labors.

This book should encourage others to pursue further improvements in the selection, propagation, and culture of laurel. A better understanding of the genetics of the species and the inheritance of specific traits will lead to cultivars only dreamed of today—perhaps to some not yet even imagined.

2 Laurels in the Wild*

Among the dwarfer evergreens there are few that rank higher in merit than the Kalmias. There are altogether seven species known, but of these only three appear to be in cultivation, all of which are valuable as garden shrubs. The genus is purely an American one, extending from arctic regions in the north as far as Cuba in the south. The tallest growing . . . is commonly known as Mountain Laurel, and is one of the chief favorites among the many plants suggested for the national flower of the United States. (Bean 1897)

The laurels, a small group of interesting and beautiful shrubs, are still relatively unknown, even though some of them were used by the early colonists and the Indians before them. Botanists recognize seven species of laurel and group them in the genus *Kalmia*. All are native to North America. These plants, which have adorned yards and gardens in the eastern United States since colonial times,

*Dr. John E. Ebinger, Eastern Illinois University, Charleston, Illinois.

7

deserve rediscovery, for improved horticultural forms have gone virtually unnoticed and unused. Mountain laurel, *Kalmia latifolia*, is the best known species and is considered by many to be the most beautiful flowering shrub in North America. This explains why it is highly prized as an ornamental (Figure 2–1).

References to mountain laurel are found in early colonial litera- ture. Possibly the "rose-trees" in Henry Hudson's log of his 1609 trip to Cape Cod were this species. Captain John Smith observed the occurrence of laurel as an understory shrub in Virginia in 1624. By the early 1700s a few species of the genus had been described and illustrated in some of the botanical works of the colonies.

One of the first detailed accounts of laurels is found in Peter Kalm's journal. This Swedish botanist, a student of Linnaeus, was sent to the New World in 1748 by the Swedish Academy of Science. His mission was to obtain seeds of plants hardy enough to thrive on Swedish soil and in particular to discover dye-plants, new food

Figure 2–1   Mountain laurel, *Kalmia latifolia*, is the state flower of Connecticut and Pennsylvania and is a candidate for the national flower of the United States.

and fodder crops, and hardy mulberry trees to develop a silk industry. During his three years in America his explorations extended through Pennsylvania, New York, and New Jersey and into southern Canada. He ventured as far west as Niagara Falls and was the first man to describe the falls in English from first-hand observations. Although primarily a naturalist who made numerous observations of plants and animals, he also made many valuable observations of the colonists themselves. Thus his journal, written after his return to Europe, is an interesting account of life in colonial times: how the people lived, what they ate and drank, how they dressed, the native plants they used, and what they learned from the Indians. In this journal he describes in detail the poisonous properties of the "Laurel Trees." He also discusses the characteristics, economic importance, habitat requirements, and general distribution of mountain laurel and sheep laurel, *Kalmia angustifolia*.

Upon his return to Europe, Kalm gave his collection of about 380 species of plants to Carolus Linnaeus, the Swedish naturalist and taxonomist. It was from this material that Linnaeus published a dissertation in which he proposed the generic name *Kalmia* to honor the collector. In this publication both mountain laurel, *K. latifolia*, and sheep laurel, *K. angustifolia*, were named and distinguished from other related genera and species. Linnaeus included both in his *Species Plantarum* (1753), making the names official. Of the 700 species of North American plants described by Linnaeus in the *Species Plantarum*, Kalm was mentioned as the collector of many, with at least 60 new species founded upon specimens he collected.

The use of laurels as ornamentals in colonial gardens was well established when Peter Kalm was in America; in fact, some species were already being used as ornamentals in Europe. Twelve years before his visit, living specimens of both mountain laurel and sheep laurel had been sent to Peter Collinson, a London merchant, by American naturalist John Bartram. Other reports in 1740 tell of mountain laurel flowering in England. A third species, the eastern bog laurel, *K. polifolia*, made its way to England by 1767. As a result of these beginnings numerous European horticultural forms have been developed, and some of these have found their way back to America.

The genus *Kalmia* is regarded as a relatively primitive member (in an evolutionary sense) of the heath family (Ericaceae). This family occurs mainly throughout most of the temperate zone with some species found in the mountains of the tropics and others in sub-arctic regions. It includes a great variety of plants, most of them shrubs and subshrubs, some herbs, others fairly tall trees, and a few trailing vines. The family contains about 2500 species; the largest genera are the true heaths (*Erica*), the rhododendrons and azaleas (*Rhododendron*), the wintergreens (*Gaultheria*), and the blue-berries and cranberries (*Vaccinium*).

Economically the family is important primarily for its many orna-mental species; among them the most popular are the azaleas and rhododendrons. The evergreen mountain laurel and rhododendron species are popular greens in the floral industry especially at Christ-mas, and of course blueberries and cranberries are an ever popular source of food.

BOTANICAL CHARACTERISTICS OF LAUREL
The laurels are a purely North American genus occurring from Alaska south to the mountains of California and Utah, east through Canada to the Atlantic Ocean and south through the eastern United States to Florida and Cuba. All of the species are low to medium-sized shrubs or rarely small trees, usually with leathery, evergreen, entire margined, mostly short-petioled leaves (Figure 2–2) that are alternate, opposite, or whorled. In some species the flowers are solitary in the axils of the leaves, while in others they are in terminal or axillary clusters. The flowers are relatively large, varying from ¼ to 1 inch in width. The calyx is five-parted and is usually persistent in fruit. The shallow, five-lobed petals are fused into a saucer-shaped corolla with a short narrow tube. Each has ten small pouches holding the anthers. The ten stamens have slender fila-ments, and anthers that open by apical slits. The five-celled ovary is superior, while the fruit consists of a globose capsule holding numerous small seeds.

The most distinctive feature of the genus *Kalmia* is the pollen-discharge mechanism. Near the middle of the corolla are ten pouches forming small lobes on each ridge of the flower bud (Figure 2–2, A and B). Just before the bud opens, the elongating filaments push the anthers upward into these pouches. As the corolla opens, the

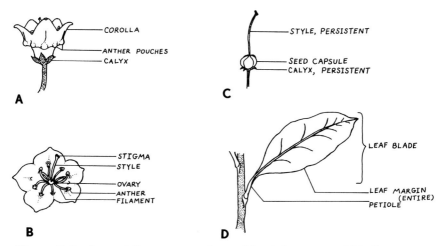

Figure 2-2   Laurel flower, capsule, and leaf diagrams: (A) flower in profile, (B) face view, (C) developed seed capsule before splitting to release seeds, (D) stem and leaf.

elastic filaments bend backward under tension, and the anthers are held in the pouches and carried down and outward. When the flower is disturbed by a large insect, one or more of the anthers is released. When this occurs, the tension of the elastic filament is strong enough to throw the pollen 3 to 6 inches from the flower. Many early botanists thought this mechanism insured self-pollination, because the pollen was thrown toward the stigma of the flower. American botanist and horticulturalist Dr. William J. Beal was probably the first person to report that cross-pollination was necessary for pollination in the laurel species and was the first to describe the way in which cross-pollination occurred. He observed that a bumblebee searching around the base of the flower would release the stamens with his proboscis, thereby projecting the pollen onto the underside of his body. This pollen was then rubbed onto the stigmas of subsequently visited flowers.

The flowers of laurel do not readily attract insects, although they are necessary for pollination. In fact, casual observations might lead to the conclusion that no insect pollination occurs. Furthermore, little nectar is secreted at the base of the corolla tube, and none can be found in many flowers, apparently accounting for the comparatively small number of insect visitors. But closer observation now reveals that insects are indeed necessary for pollination in laurels. This can be verified by preventing insects access to the flower clusters. In flowers thus isolated, none of the stamens is released from the pouches and no seed is produced. Also, most species of laurel are self-incompatible, producing almost no seeds when self-pollination does occur. On the rare occasion when pollination does occur, the seedlings show inbreeding depression and are small and slow growing. In fact, measured by height growth, the vigor of outcrossed seedlings is usually twice that of inbred seedlings.

Compared with other insect-pollinated plants, few species of insects have been observed pollinating laurel. In one study, a population of sheep laurel in an abandoned pasture in Maine was observed for three weeks to determine the agents of pollination. Fourteen species of insects were identified with the ability to spring the stamens while foraging for nectar. Of these, the bumblebee, *Bombus ternarius*, and the mining bee, *Andrena vicina*, were the most common visitors. Other insects observed visiting the flowers occasionally included smaller bees of the superfamily Apoides, three butterflies, one hawkmoth, and one beetle. During the study no honeybees, *Apis* sp., were observed even though an apiary was located only a third of a mile away. Present information suggests that under normal conditions honeybees rarely visit the laurels.

Bumblebees are by far the most important pollination agent, because these large insects easily spring the stamens while foraging for nectar. As they alight on the flowers, their ventral parts touch the projecting stigma. But in most instances the stamens are not released when the bee lands but are sprung by the insect's legs (which get caught under the filaments) or by the insect's proboscis as it searches for the nectar. The proboscis is inserted near the base of the flower between the filaments and the corolla tube, and in a single circular motion probes completely around the base of the ovary. This liberates all the stamens, projecting the pollen onto the underside of the insect. After being sprung, the stamens remain erect and in contact with the style for two or three hours; then the filaments bend backward and the anthers rest on the corolla.

In most flowering plants, the pollen grains are produced in tetrads (groups of four) as a result of meiosis, and these four cells develop into separate and distinct pollen grains. In the genus *Kalmia*, as well as in many other members of the family Ericaceae, however, these four cells remain united at maturity and are released from the anther as a single unit. These four-celled, compound pollen grains are released as a fine powder in some species of *Kalmia* and in others as a sticky net formed by the presence of fine, noncellular, tacky threads which hold the tetrads together. These threads are derived either from small quantities of protoplasm excluded from the tetrads during development or from the breakdown of elements in the tetrad's outer wall. They have been observed in mountain laurel, sandhill laurel, and the little known *Kalmia ericoides*, which grows only in Cuba. The function of these threads is not known, but they may facilitate pollination in the relatively large, upright flowers found in these species.

THE FOSSIL RECORD

Four extinct species of *Kalmia* have been described, but their fossil remains are extremely fragmentary. As a result it is difficult to form definite conclusions concerning their relationship to present-day members of the genus. Three fossil species are known only from leaf impressions, and, except for size, shape, and probable coriaceous (leathery) texture, there is little reason to consider them members of this genus. They vary in age from Upper Cretaceous to Miocene and were found in various locations throughout North America. The fourth species, *Kalmia saxonica*, from the Lower Miocene period of Europe, may represent a member of this genus or of a closely related genus of the Ericaceae. The remains of this species consist of pieces of leaf cuticle with some upper epidermis attached. The structure and arrangement of the cells and the type of glandular hair bases are similar to that found in present-day mountain laurel.

One present-day species is suspected to have existed from scant fossil evidence. Fossils of the eastern bog laurel, *K. polifolia*, were first reported from interglacial deposits at Point Grey near Vancouver, British Columbia. The leaf impressions are the same shape and size as those of living bog laurel. This species was later reported from Pleistocene lake deposits of the upper Connecticut River valley in northern New Hampshire. These fossils are postglacial in age and appear to be representative of the flora that migrated northward in the wake of the retreating Wisconsin ice sheet. The other fossils in the same deposits indicate a habitat and climate similar to that presently prevailing in the area. Positive identification of these leaf impressions as bog laurel is impossible because of the similarity of the leaves of many Ericaceae.

THE SPECIES OF LAUREL

The genus *Kalmia* consists of seven species. For the most part they are quite distinctive, and no problem is encountered in identifying them. A description of each of these species follows with their general range, habitat, and economic importance. Descriptions are also included of the varieties and forms that are sometimes encountered in the wild.

Western Laurel, *Kalmia microphylla*

This short alpine plant is sparsely branched, grows up to 2 feet tall, and has slightly two-edged branchlets. The leaves are opposite, leathery, flat, evergreen, ovate to oval, short-petioled, and ¼ to 1½ inches long. The midrib of the leaf lacks glandular hairs, and the leaf margins are not revolute. The inflorescence is a few-flowered terminal raceme (simple arrangement of stalked flowers on an elongated stem); the flowers on slender stalks grow to 1 inch long. Flowering is in late spring or early summer. The individual flowers are rose purple to pink, and ¼ to ¾ inch across. The fruit is a globose capsule; the seeds have short projections on each end.

The western laurel is the only species of the genus found west of the Rocky Mountains. It extends from central California north to Alaska and east to the extreme northwest corner of Manitoba (Figure 2–3). This low-growing alpine shrub rarely exceeds 6 inches in height, but in bogs at lower elevations it may reach a height of 2 feet. The species contains two varieties, the western alpine laurel, *K. microphylla* var. *microphylla*, and the western swamp laurel, *K. microphylla* var. *occidentalis*.

The two varieties are distinct in habit and general appearance. The western alpine laurel rarely exceeds 6 inches in height and has small oval leaves usually less than ½ inch long. Its flowers are relatively small. The western swamp laurel, in contrast, is a larger plant growing up to 2 feet tall with lanceolate leaves ½ to 1½ inches long and slightly larger flowers.

Botanical Key to Species of Laurel

---

a. Leaves opposite

  b. Midrib of leaves lacking stalked glands; seeds less than 1/16 inch (1.5 mm) long

                          Western laurel, *K. microphylla*

  b. Midrib of leaves with stalked glands; seeds more than 1/16 inch (1.5 mm)

                          Eastern bog laurel, *K. polifolia*

a. Leaves alternate or in whorls.

  c. Leaves mostly more than ¾ inch (2 cm) broad; inflorescence terminal, much branched

                          Mountain laurel, *K. latifolia*

  c. Leaves mostly less than ¾ inch (2 cm) broad; flowers solitary or in racemes in the axils of the leaves

    d. Leaves more than ⅝ inch (1.5 cm) long; flowers in racemes

      e. Leaves in whorls of three, evergreen

                              Sheep laurel, *K. angustifolia*

      e. Leaves alternate, deciduous

                              White wicky, *K. cuneata*

    d. Leaves less than ⅝ inch (1.5 cm) long; flowers usually solitary in the axils of the leaves

      f. Leaves broad, flat, margins only slightly rolled under

                              Sandhill laurel, *K. hirsuta*

      f. Leaves narrow, margins strongly rolled under

                              Cuban laurel, *K. ericoides*

WESTERN ALPINE LAUREL, VAR. *microphylla* Commonly called the alpine laurel or the small-leaved kalmia, this species is found in alpine meadows, bogs, and other open, wet areas where it usually forms dense mats. It is distributed throughout the mountainous regions of western North America from central California, Nevada,

Utah, and Colorado, north through the Rocky Mountains to the Yukon and the Northwest Territories (Figure 2–3). There are some reports of its occurrence north of the Arctic Circle.

Plant and leaf size in western alpine laurel are controlled to some extent by the environment. In the typical alpine plants the leaves are extremely small, usually about ½ inch long; the entire plant may be less than 3 inches tall (Figure 2–4). At lower elevations the leaves average about ½ inch in length and the plants 6 inches in height. Larger individuals are rarely found.

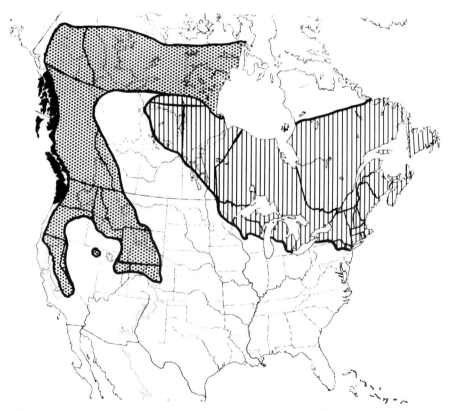

Figure 2–3 The natural range of eastern bog laurel, *Kalmia polifolia* (vertical shading); western alpine laurel, *K. microphylla* var. *microphylla* (dotted area); and western swamp laurel, *K. microphylla* var. *occidentalis* (black area).

Figure 2-4 Western alpine laurel, *Kalmia microphylla* var. *microphylla*, from the Cascade Mountains of Oregon. Total plant height with flowers of this high-altitude form is about 2 inches.

WESTERN SWAMP LAUREL, VAR. *occidentalis* Sometimes called the western bog laurel, this variety is found in marshes, bogs, and wet open areas at low elevations from coastal regions and islands of southern Alaska, British Columbia, Washington, and northwestern Oregon.

Eastern Bog Laurel, *Kalmia polifolia*

Common names for this species include bog laurel, swamp laurel, pale laurel, and gold withy. This low, sparsely branched, straggling shrub grows less than 3 feet tall with leathery, linear to oblong, evergreen, opposite, short-petioled leaves that are ½ to 1½ inches long (Figure 2–5). The midrib of the leaf is covered with small, purple, glandular hairs, while the leaf margins are usually revolute (rolled under). The inflorescence is a few-flowered terminal raceme with the flowers on slender stalks about 1 inch long. Flowering is early in the growing season.

The individual flowers are usually rose purple and ½ to ¾ inch across. The fruit is a globose capsule, and the small seeds have projections on each end.

The eastern bog laurel is found in swamps and other wet places, usually forming a border around ponds and lakes. In bogs, its roots

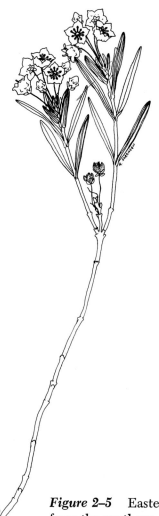

Figure 2–5   Eastern bog laurel, *Kalmia polifolia*. Plants from the southern part of the range, such as this one from Connecticut, characteristically have a lanky growth habit. Northern plants are more compact.

form dense mats that extend out over the water. Also found at higher elevations in the mountains of northeastern United States and Canada, this species is the most widely distributed member of the genus (Figure 2–3). It ranges from northeastern Alberta, across Canada to the east coast, and south into the United States. In the Great Lakes region this species extends as far south as northern Illinois and on the east coast as far south as central New Jersey. Its entire range is, however, hard to determine with certainty. The two reports of its occurrence in the Arctic Circle now appear to have been based on specimens of the western laurel, *K. microphylla.* The species is naturalized in Europe, being reported from a bog in Scotland.

The eastern bog laurel and the western laurel are similar and are often considered together as one highly variable species. Recent genetic studies now confirm, however, that they should be considered separate species. When considered thus, the plant and leaf size are used to make the distinction. (The eastern bog laurel is larger by at least a foot; its leaves are ½ to 1½ inches long, and the leaf margins are strongly revolute. Western laurel, in contrast, is most often a mere 6 inches tall, and its leaves are less than ½ inch long and have nonrevolute margins. Usually these characteristics are enough to distinguish the two species.) The most reliable characteristic, however, that separates the eastern bog laurel from the western is the presence of purple glandular hairs of the leaf midrib of the former. Another way is to compare the seeds. Those of the eastern bog laurel are about twice as long as those of the western.

A white-flowered form, *leucantha*, of the eastern bog laurel has been found growing along with the typical rose purple flowered form in a bog in Newfoundland.

Mountain Laurel, *Kalmia latifolia*

Other common names include broad-leaved laurel, calico-bush, spoonwood, ivy, mountain ivy, big-leaved ivy, laurel-leaves, and calmoun. The leaves of this many-branched shrub are alternate, flat, leathery, elliptic, dark green above, light green to reddish below, petioled, 2 to 5 inches long and less than 2 inches wide. The inflorescence consists of a terminal compound corymb (convex flower cluster with the outer flowers opening first) with glandular and mostly sticky stalks and numerous flowers. Flowering is usually in late spring or early summer after new shoot growth has begun. The calyx is green to reddish and usually has stalked glandular hairs, while the corolla, up to 1 inch across, is usually light pink with purple spots around each anther pocket. The fruit is a depressed globose capsule with numerous light brown seeds with short projections on each end.

Mountain laurel commonly forms dense thickets in rocky and sandy forests throughout most of its range, particularly where there are openings in the canopy. It is also found in pastures and open fields and often forms thickets at the edges of roads. This species is restricted to the eastern United States and occurs from southern Maine, west through southern New York to central Ohio, south to southern Mississippi, Alabama, and Georgia, and northwestern Florida (Figure 2–6). There are some reports of mountain laurel being native to Canada, but there is no conclusive, supporting evidence. Possibly these reports were based on cultivated plants or on large-leaved specimens of the more northern sheep laurel, *K. angustifolia.*

Mountain laurel is usually a tall, spreading shrub that throughout most of its range rarely exceeds a height of 12 feet. Yet in the

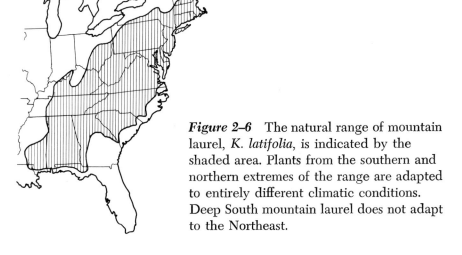

Figure 2–6   The natural range of mountain laurel, *K. latifolia,* is indicated by the shaded area. Plants from the southern and northern extremes of the range are adapted to entirely different climatic conditions. Deep South mountain laurel does not adapt to the Northeast.

fertile Blue Ridge valleys and in the Allegheny Mountains members of this species may attain the size of a small tree. In 1877 American botanist Asa Gray observed a number of large individuals growing in the bottom of a dell, in back of Caesar's Head, on the extreme western border of South Carolina. One of the trunks, at a point 1 foot above ground, measured 4 feet, 1¼ inches in circumference. Another in the same area, measured 3 feet, 4 inches above the first fork and at 1 foot above the ground, was 4 feet, 4 inches in circumference. The largest specimen listed by the American Forestry Association is a plant located at Fannin City, Georgia. This specimen measured at a point 4½ feet above ground is 4½ feet in circumference. It has a spread of 28 feet and is 20 feet tall (Figure 2–7).

Like most members of the family Ericaceae, mountain laurel is dependent on a mycorrhizal fungus association with its roots. This symbiotic relationship insures adequate absorption of water and minerals by the plant, particularly in acid soils. Some members of the family are so dependent on this association that they have lost the ability to make their own food. This condition is well known in the nongreen Indian pipe, *Monotropa uniflora*, and a number of its relatives.

Economically, the mountain laurel is the most important member of the genus *Kalmia*. The species is sold as an ornamental, particularly in the eastern United States. The foliage is also used for floral displays and Christmas decorations, continuing a tradition started in colonial times. Suggestions were made early in 1913 that the species should be protected against indiscriminate collecting. In 1924, 1,000 tons of mountain laurel foliage was estimated as the amount used annually in New York City alone. The estimate for the United States exceeded 10,000 tons. No figures are presently available for decorative use of mountain laurel, nor do we know if significant amounts are still used to produce a yellow dye.

The wood of mountain laurel was occasionally used to make small items such as pipes where it was a substitute for brier. Peter Kalm mentioned in his journal that this strong wood was fashioned into weaver's shuttles, pulleys, and trowels. American Indians used the wood for small dishes and spoons, which probably accounts for the common name *spoonwood*. Today the wood is rarely used except for tool handles and novelties.

Mountain laurel, as an understory shrub, effectively prevents

Figure 2-7 A giant mountain laurel growing with rhododendron in the Chattahoochee National Forest, Georgia, near the border of North Carolina and Tennessee. This national champion mountain laurel, found by G. C. Hoffman, is listed in the American Forestry Association's *Social Register of Big Trees* (1973). The base of the plant is more than 4 feet in diameter. About 2½ feet up, it branches into three major stems, two of them living. The largest stem is over 17 inches in diameter, 4½ feet from the ground. (Size can be judged by the 1-foot ruler and hard hat. Photo by Tony Durkas, U.S. Forest Service.)

water runoff and soil erosion. Studies in the southern Appalachian Mountains have shown that excessive cutting of dense laurel stands greatly increased the amount of water runoff. Since dense thickets of mountain laurel also prevent the natural regeneration of timber trees, the thickets must be cleared before the desirable tree species are planted.

Because of the many variations in flower color, leaf shape and size, plant size, and pubescence, several variants and forms of mountain laurel have been named (Figure 2–8). A number of these represent the normal range of variation of the population and should be

Figure 2–8 Mountain laurel from the northern part of the range (*top*) has a more compact inflorescence than plants originating from the southern part (*bottom*). Sticky glandular hairs are abundant on the flower pedicels (stalks) of northern plants and are nearly absent from those of the extreme southern part.

treated as cultivars.* At least five, however, are true genetic variants that are distinguished by one or several linked characters from the normal populations and are designated botanical forms:

WILLOW-LEAVED MOUNTAIN LAUREL, FORM *angustata*   First reported in Cape May County, New Jersey, this rare foliage form exhibits very narrow, willow-shaped leaves less than ½ inch wide (Figure 2–9a).

MINIATURE MOUNTAIN LAUREL, FORM *myrtifolia*   Also called dwarf mountain laurel, this form has been under cultivation since 1840 and is occasionally found in small gardens. It is in all respects a miniature mountain laurel, compact, slow-growing, and rarely exceeding a height of 3 feet (Figure 2–9b). The leaves are generally smaller than those of typical mountain laurel, averaging ½ to 1½ inches long and about ½ inch wide. Flower size and the length of the stem internodes are one-third to one-half those of normal laurel.

HEDGE MOUNTAIN LAUREL, FORM *obtusata*   First found near Pomfret, Connecticut, this rare foliage form has oval leaves. The leaves are usually 1 to 2½ inches long and up to 1½ inches wide. Most specimens are slow growing and form compact plants (Figure 2–9c).

BANDED MOUNTAIN LAUREL, FORM *fuscata*   Also called the crowned mountain laurel, this flower color form has been reported from many localities in the northeastern United States. Its white to pink flowers have a heavily pigmented, usually continuous, brownish purple or cinnamon band on the inside of the corolla at the level of the anther pockets (Figure 2–10). This band breaks up into brownish dots toward the base and the margin of the corolla. Because it shows through the bud, the corolla often has a muddy appearance. Variation exists in the size, shape, and color of the band with an interrupted band having been observed in some individuals.

---

* Cultivar is the generally accepted term to designate single plant selections of horticultural merit that received fancy names (e.g., 'Pink Surprise') and are vegetatively propagated. The term variety may be used the same way but it is used here only in the botanical sense, as a subdivision of a species.

Figure 2-9   Three foliage forms of mountain laurel. (A) 'Willowcrest', a willow-leafed form, previously unnamed, having flowing, strap-shaped, attractive leaves. The flowers are typical for the species. ('Willowcrest' is believed to have been collected in the wild in North Carolina by Richard Pohl. A large plant grows on the grounds of the Henry Foundation for Botanical Research, Gladwyne, Pennsylvania.) (B) A compact seedling, hedge laurel, with near-normal-sized leaves. (C) The miniature or *myrtifolia* form, which by appropriate crosses can be obtained from seed. (All three photos taken from above and at the same magnification.)

FEATHER PETAL MOUNTAIN LAUREL, FORM *polypetala*   Found on Mt. Toby, near South Deerfield, Massachusetts, this form has also been found growing wild in North Carolina. The corolla is deeply divided into five narrow to broad petals (Figure 2–11, left). In some in-

Figure 2–10   The banded mountain laurel, form *fuscata*, seen here is only occasionally found in the wild.

dividuals the extremely narrow and thread-like petals are caused by a rolling of the petal margin. Normally the petals are broader, and a few specimens have been found with flowers like apple blossoms. Other variations are mere extensions of the polypetala type or may be distinct forms. One lacks petals altogether, apetala, (Figure 2–11, right) and a cultivar in which the corolla is reduced in size and deeply lobed has been named 'Bettina' by T. R. Dudley of the National Arboretum.

Sheep Laurel, *Kalmia angustifolia*

This many-branched shrub may grow 6 feet tall and has reddish brown branchlets. The leaves in whorls of three are somewhat leathery, evergreen, flat, mostly oblong, and 1 to 2½ inches long. The leaves and stems are slightly hairy and have stalked glandular hairs on their surfaces. The flowers are borne in numerous small clusters from the axils of last year's leaves (Figure 2–12). The blooming period is generally June, about the same time as mountain laurel. The calyx is usually

Figure 2–11 Two abnormal petal types in mountain laurel: *polypetala* form (*top*), with each flower usually having five petals; *apetala* form (*bottom*), an extreme condition in which the corolla, or petals, are lacking entirely.

Figure 2–12   Sheep laurel, *Kalmia angustifolia.*

green with red tips or red throughout, while the corolla is less than
½ inch across and reddish purple to pink. The fruit is composed of a
depressed globose capsule with numerous small, yellowish seeds
that have two short wings.

The sheep laurel is common in northeastern and eastern North
America (Figure 2–13). John K. Small, an American botanist who
studied the flora of the southeastern United States, classified it as
two separate species.* Most botanists, however, consider the sheep
laurel complex as being one species with two fairly distinct varieties.

* Southall and Hardin (1974) in a recent study have also treated sheep laurel as two
  separate species.

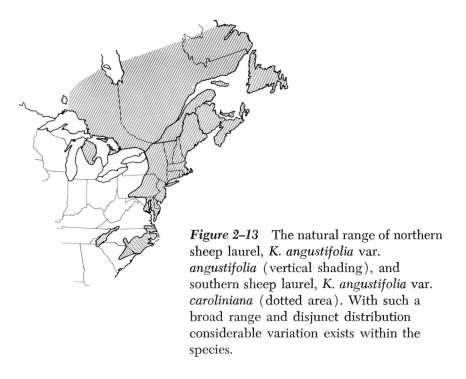

Figure 2–13 The natural range of northern sheep laurel, *K. angustifolia* var. *angustifolia* (vertical shading), and southern sheep laurel, *K. angustifolia* var. *caroliniana* (dotted area). With such a broad range and disjunct distribution considerable variation exists within the species.

The genetic and morphological similarities make it more realistic to follow this latter view. Therefore, we treat this species as the northern sheep laurel, *K. angustifolia* var. *angustifolia,* and the southern sheep laurel, *K. angustifolia* var. *caroliniana.* The two varieties are similar in habit and general appearance but are easily distinguished by differences in leaf and calyx pubescence. In the northern sheep laurel the calyx is densely glandular pubescent (small hairs), and the leaves are glabrous (hairless). The southern sheep laurel has no glandular hairs on the calyx, and the leaves are densely pubescent beneath with a mat of extremely short hairs.

NORTHERN SHEEP LAUREL, VAR. *angustifolia*   Common names for this variety include lambkill, sheepkill, wicky, narrow-leaved kalmia, dwarf laurel, and pig laurel. It occurs in bogs, swamps, and other wet places, forming dense thickets around ponds and lakes, and in open woods, as a weed in pastures, and in the moist openings of pine savannas. It is distributed from the northeastern part of the

Michigan peninsula and the eastern half of Ontario, east through Quebec, the Maritime provinces, and Newfoundland; north to the Attawapiskat River (Kenora District) in Ontario, and to Goose Bay and Cartwright in Labrador; and south in the eastern United States through New England and eastern New York, eastern Pennsylvania and Maryland, to the coast in New Jersey and Delaware, and the southeastern tip of Virginia.

Most of the subspecific categories proposed for the northern sheep laurel are for variations and extremes in flower color, variation in size and habit, and variation in leaf shape and color. In general, the differences in flower color represent natural variation within populations and should be treated as cultivars. The variation in leaf shape and color, and, in part, variation in plant height, should be treated the same way. Variation in plant height is the result of selection of more northern or high-altitude sources, or the result of inbreeding depression.

A white flowered form, *candida*, of the northern sheep laurel was first reported from Newfoundland in 1915 and has now been observed in a few other locations in Canada and the northeastern United States. The presence of pigment in sheep laurel is controlled by a single dominant gene, and the true-breeding recessive is white-flowered. These white-flowered individuals also have green stems, unlike the normal wild types which have reddish stems.

SOUTHERN SHEEP LAUREL, VAR. *caroliniana*   This variety is common in North Carolina and occurs in open woods and shrubby bogs in the mountains, in sandy woods, pocosins (marsh or swamp), savannas, and bogs on the coastal plain.

Sporadic occurrence has been reported on the coastal plains of South Carolina and southern Virginia and in a few locations in the mountains of eastern Tennessee and two mountain bogs in the Blue Ridge of northeastern Georgia.

A white-flowered form of the southern sheep laurel also exists. It is similar genetically to the white-flowered form of the northern sheep laurel in that the true-breeding recessive is white-flowered. The only known plants of this form come from Garden in the Woods, Framingham, Massachusetts. No wild individuals have been observed, and the origin of the nursery material is unknown.

White Wicky, *Kalmia cuneata*

One of the rarest shrubs in North America, this many-branched, erect shrub may become 5 feet tall. The leaves are alternate, deciduous, thin and flat, petioled, oblanceolate (lance-shaped but broadest near the apex) and 1 to 2½ inches long. Stalked glandular hairs are scattered over most parts of the plant. The flowers are borne in clusters of three to ten in the upper axils of the previous year's growth. Flowering is in early spring before new foliage and shoots expand. The corolla is ½ to ¾ inch across and creamy white with a red band within. The fruit is a depressed globose capsule on a recurved stalk. The light brown seeds are small.

White wicky is a distinctive species (Figure 2–14). It could only

Figure 2–14   White wicky, *Kalmia cuneata.*

Figure 2–15   The natural range of white wicky, *K. cuneata* (dotted area); and sandhill laurel, *K. hirsuta* (vertical shading). Despite limited geographic distribution, there exists within each species considerable variation for plant form and flower color.

be confused with the sheep laurel, since their general habitat and leaf size are similar. White wicky, however, is the only deciduous member of the genus. It is found only in wet thickets and shrub bogs of the pocosin ecotone in eight counties of southeastern North Carolina and adjacent South Carolina (Figure 2–15). These sites are marshy upland areas of the coastal plain in between two ecological zones.

Sandhill Laurel, *Kalmia hirsuta*

Sometimes called calico-bush, this species is a low, lightly branched shrub less than 2 feet tall with alternate, commonly short-petioled, elliptic to ovate leaves less than ½ inch long with margins only slightly revolute. The leaves and stems are covered with short, densely packed hairs as well as scattered, long coarse hairs and stalked glandular hairs. The flowers are usually solitary in the axils of the leaves of new growth (Figure 2–16). The blooming period is extended, often from early summer until fall. The calyx is green, leaf-like, and tardily deciduous in fruit. The corolla is about ½ inch across and light pink with red markings around the anther pockets and a red ring near its base. The fruit is a subglobose capsule covered with glandular hairs and containing numerous light brown seeds.

The sandhill laurel has a relatively limited distribution, occurring along the coastal plain in the southeastern United States (Figure 2–15). It has been observed from extreme southern Alabama and

Figure 2–16   Sandhill laurel, *Kalmia hirsuta*.

northern Florida and north through Georgia to the southeastern tip of South Carolina. Usually found in low, sandy pine savannas, sandhills, dunes and flat relatively open pine woods, this low-growing plant forms clumps among the understory. It does extremely well in sunny areas and is found in pine woods openings caused by logging or burning.

Horticultural variants of sandhill laurel have not been described in the literature, but Tom Dodd of Semmes, Alabama, observed a colony of sandhill laurel with hose-in-hose (double-cupped) flowers while on a field trip in southeastern Georgia. This trait would be of great ornamental value in cultivated laurels. Sandhill laurels with banded or fuscata type flowers have also been observed.

Cuban Laurel, *Kalmia ericoides*

Sparsely branched, this erect to spreading shrub sometimes reaches a height of 3 feet. The leaves are alternate, persistent, thick, leathery, subsessile (virtually no petiole), linear, about ½ inch long with strongly revolute margins. Most of the plant is covered with short, densely packed hairs, scattered, long coarse hairs, and well-developed stalked glandular hairs. The flowers are solitary in the axils of the leaves near the ends of the branches, forming tight terminal clusters. The calyx is green, leaf-like, and tardily deciduous in fruit. The corolla is about ½ inch across and light pink with red markings around the anther pockets and a red ring near the base. The fruit is a subglobose capsule covered with glandular hairs and containing numerous reddish brown seeds.

The Cuban laurel is endemic to the savannas and pine barrens of western Cuba. Though it has a very limited distribution, the variation that exists in leaf pubescence and in the compactness of the inflorescence has caused this species to be divided into three species by some botanists, while others have considered it a single highly variable species. It now appears that the compactness of the inflorescence is not a completely reliable characteristic. The variation in leaf pubescence, however, is relatively stable; two varieties do probably exist in this complex.

The Cuban laurel appears to be most closely related to the sandhill laurel of the southeastern United States. Both have relatively small leaves (about ½ inch long), covered with long coarse hairs and stalked glandular hairs. Their flowers are borne singly in the axils of the leaves, and the calyx is leafy and tardily deciduous in fruit. The two are easily separated, however, since the leaves of the Cuban laurel are thick and leathery with strongly revolute margins, while in the sandhill laurel the leaves are thin and lack a strongly revolute margin. Also, the flowers are borne scattered along the stem in the sandhill laurel; in the Cuban laurel they are found toward the end of the stem, giving the appearance of a terminal cluster.

3

Selections Worthy of Propagation

The mountain laurel is one of the most beautiful of evergreen shrubs. It grows commonly in the shade of the forest, where its shiny leaves add a strong note of dark green to the paler greens of the summer woods. In winter its dark foliage shows boldly against the snows of the north and the bare browns of the leafless southern woods. In June it rises to the height of its glory, when it is covered with great clusters of pink flowers which give a rose-like glow to the whole underwood. (Buttrick 1924)

Here is a pictorial account of the more colorful laurels (Color Plate Figures 1–20). And here a few of the outstanding ones are given cultivar (variety) names for the first time. Hopefully many of these selections will soon be available to gardeners. The emphasis is on varieties of mountain laurel, but remember that considerable variation exists in the other species as well. Twenty-five distinct traits of mountain laurel are known (Table 13–1) without even counting the more subtle variations and recombinations. If recombinant types were considered, such as a banded red-bud or a miniature 'Shooting Star', then the varieties of mountain laurel would be counted in the hundreds. Imagine the flower color series of mountain laurel as it presently exists transferred into plants of dwarf stature, or these color forms incorporated into plants with petaled flowers or willow-like leaves. Clearly many striking recombinants are possible.

Considering the unusual forms recently found in the wild, we can assume that others with horticultural value are yet to be discovered. Perhaps a mountain laurel with a solid red flower may arise, or one with a hose-in-hose, or any other permutation may be discovered or bred in time.

CULTIVAR NAMES

The great temptation to give cultivar names to every distinct and beautiful laurel should be resisted. To give in is to fill the literature with colorful names but not to create any more colorful plants for the garden. So, common sense dictates that only those plants tested at more than one location, and preferably only those under propagation, should be named. Indeed, plant scientists have developed rules for the naming of plant cultivars, the International Code of Nomenclature for Cultivated Plants. This code prescribes that the name of each clone (cultivar) be no longer than two words, that it should not contain initials, numerals, or abbreviations, that it should not imply exaggerated merit, and, to avoid confusion, that it should not duplicate an existing name in a closely related group. Once established, the name of the clone may not be changed.

More red-budded or pink-flowered clones need not be named until they are in commercial propagation; however, I do not consider this rule inflexible. Occasionally a plant turns up that is so different from anything seen before that its popularization with a name is warranted. The newly found 'Shooting Star' was named within three years of its discovery in the wild, because a laurel of this pleasing flower form had never before been reported (Color Plate Figure 10). Another selection named here for the first time is 'Goodrich', a banded laurel with a band so wide it virtually fills the inside of the cup (Color Plate Figure 7). Other new cultivars are mountain laurels 'Pink Surprise', 'Stillwood', and 'Willowcrest'; sheep laurel 'Ham-

1. Red-budded mountain laurel makes a spectacular calico bush, yet it is also simple and exquisite. Most intense coloration is found in plants grown in full sun.

2. Wild or normal form of mountain laurel with strong pink blush to buds.

3. 'Stillwood' is a nearly pure white
mountain laurel from New Hampshire.
The buds are white with very faint
markings within the corolla, even when
plant is grown in full sun.

4. 'Star-ring', a subtle but
unique variety of mountain
laurel, has five points
radiating from the bold
ring at the base of the
corolla. (Photo by Janice
Langston.)

5. A light and lively pink
mountain laurel that is
similar to the cultivar
'Brilliant' grown in Great
Britain.

6. *A native stand of mountain laurel under a canopy of trees that has been thinned and pruned to admit more light to increase flowering.*

7. *'Goodrich' is a deeply pigmented, unusually broad-banded type. This mountain laurel was selected from a native stand at Chaplin, Connecticut.*

8. This striking, full-banded mountain laurel clone with a rich cinnamon color was found by Bristol Nursery in Bristol, Connecticut.

9. A banded mountain laurel with a typical interrupted or sometimes continuous narrow band.

10. 'Shooting Star', discovered in 1971, with its deeply cut reflexed lobes, has notable ornamental value. It flowers two weeks later than normal mountain laurel. (Photo by Marjorie W. Rogers.)

11. Inheritance of red-budded flower color in mountain laurel. Each open flower and bud cluster is from a different plant. Two plants, represented by the central clusters, were crossed, and all the seedlings were red budded.

12. 'Silver Dollar' is a selection of Weston Nurseries and is one of the best large-flowered mountain laurels. The flowers are indeed the size of a silver dollar, and the leaves are large and leathery. 'Silver Dollar' may be a tetraploid or at least have an abnormal chromosome number.

13. Here is one of the most intensely colored mountain laurels in bloom. The tight cluster of flowers gives an overall look similar to a hydrangea.

14. Red-budded mountain laurel with
candy-stripe effect in the open flowers,
selected at Weston Nurseries.

15. This is a good strong
pink, accented with spots
at the anther pockets and
a bold ring at the corolla
base. This mountain laurel
clone (293) has proven to
be a good parent to obtain
deep pink flowered
seedlings.

16. 'Pumila', a compact, richly colored form of sheep laurel, is an effective ground cover. Sheep laurel normally flowers in June at about the same time as mountain laurel, but 'Pumila' has the added feature of producing flowers at the end of the growing season in the last month or two before frost.

17. Deeply pigmented forms of sheep laurel are most commonly found in the northern parts of its range. They contrast well when planted with a pure white flowered form.

18. This is a new color combination in mountain laurel, derived from the second generation of a cross of a red-budded plant with a banded. It is eye catching in bud as well as in full flower.

19. Sandhill laurel is a small-leafed species from the southeastern United States that should be looked at more closely to find good garden forms. Some selections are being propagated and tested at Tom Dodd Nurseries in Semmes, Alabama.

20. A hybrid of the eastern bog laurel and western laurel growing in a rock garden. Unlike the other laurels, these flower in early spring. This is a numbered clone (x812s); another larger growing selection (x356h) may be released under the name 'Rocky Top'.

monasset', and the eastern bog and western alpine laurel hybrid 'Rocky Top'.

Named selections should stimulate others to propagate them, whether for pleasure or profit, and to breed or find even better selections. Named cultivars provide the standard by which other potentially better plants may be measured and thus begins the evolution of improved cultivars. Laurel selections of the future should represent improvements and extensions of flower and foliage traits in plants more amenable to vegetative propagation.

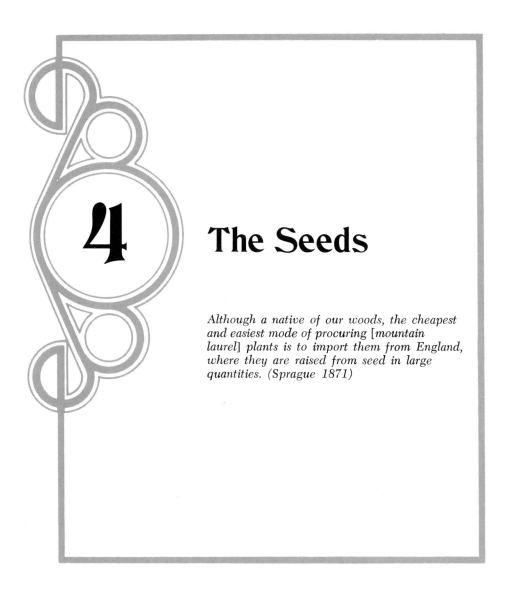

4

The Seeds

Although a native of our woods, the cheapest and easiest mode of procuring [mountain laurel] plants is to import them from England, where they are raised from seed in large quantities. (Sprague 1871)

Laurel seed is small and requires careful handling for good germination. The seed of each species has a characteristic size and shape (Figures 4–1, 4–2), and specific germination requirements. The sandhill laurel, *Kalmia hirsuta*, has the smallest seeds, as many as five million to the ounce, smaller, in fact, than petunia, tobacco, or begonia seeds.

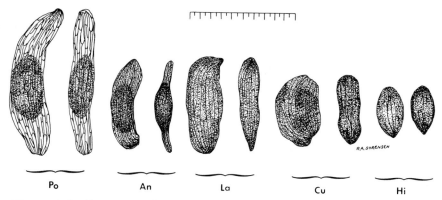

Figure 4-1 Drawings of typical seeds of five laurel species. Po, eastern bog laurel; An, sheep laurel; La, mountain laurel; Cu, white wicky; Hi, sandhill laurel. The total scale is 1 mm (1/25 inch) in length.

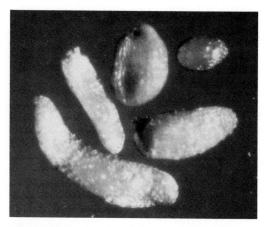

Figure 4-2 Seeds of five laurels. *Upper left*, sheep laurel; *lower left*, eastern bog laurel; *top center*, white wicky; *upper right*, sandhill laurel; *lower right*, mountain laurel.

SEED HARVEST AND CLEANING

Maturation of seed capsules even in the same area will vary by a few days from year to year. If capsules are harvested too soon, the seed will not be ripe and, even if mature enough to germinate, it may not shed readily from the capsule. As the capsules mature, they change from green to brown. If left on the plant too long, the capsule will dehisce (split) and scatter its seeds. Yet, with mountain laurel and sheep laurel it is often possible to extract a few seeds from capsules left on the plant in the spring or summer, six to nine months after they have ripened. The approximate flowering period, days to seed harvest, and harvest period for Connecticut are given in Figure 4–3. Each species is distinct from the others, either in time of flowering, time of seed harvest, period of flowering, or period required for seed maturation.

To extract small quantities of seed, place the harvested capsules in a coin envelope or other small container and allow them to dry for a few days. The capsules will then open and the seeds can be shaken loose. The seed will separate from the capsule but will be mixed with dust and chaff. Clean the seeds by gently funneling them down a trough-shaped piece of white paper and letting them fall a short distance onto another piece of paper. Repeat the process several times, and most of the chaff will separate from the seed.

Large quantities of dirty seed can be shaken through sieves

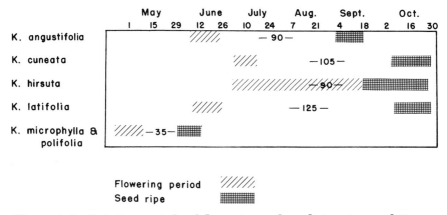

Figure 4–3 Relative periods of flowering and seed ripening, and time from flowering to seed maturation in days. The dates are for Connecticut and will vary at other locations, but the general pattern will hold. Note an almost fourfold difference in the time required for mountain laurel seed to mature as compared with bog and western laurel. It can also be seen that sandhill laurel tends to be ever-blooming.

(most mountain laurel seed will pass through a 0.5-mm round-holed sieve). Even with this method a final cleaning on white paper is recommended, because any debris left with the seed increases chances of contamination and will support fungal growth at the time of germination.

The greater specific gravity of the laurel seed also makes other cleaning methods possible. Seedsmen could use commercial air separators to winnow the heavier, viable seed from the dust and chaff. Or the fresh, filled mountain laurel seed can be placed in water, where the chaff and unfilled seeds float and the viable seeds sink to the bottom. Decant the debris and remove the good seed and dry it for sowing.

SEED STORAGE AND LONGEVITY

Laurel seed maintains its viability for several years if stored under cool, dry conditions. I store seed in glassine or coin envelopes in open trays in a household refrigerator (40°F). Exact longevity of seed for the species has not been determined. However, mountain laurel seed has shown little loss in viability through eight years of storage; after nine years, germination markedly decreased. Indeed, fresh mountain laurel seed does not germinate as well as seed stored a year or more.

GENERAL REQUIREMENTS FOR
GERMINATION AND EARLY GROWTH

The best temperature for germination and initial growth is between 70 and 75°F. Constant temperatures above 80° decrease survival, whereas temperatures below 70° will slow growth dramatically (Figure 4–4). A cool, wet germination and growing medium, especially during cloudy, low-light periods in winter may result in ammonia buildup and root injury.

Various mixes can be used for germination, including pure peat moss or ground sphagnum moss. I prefer the following for small batches of seed germinated in closed, but not airtight, plastic boxes (proportions by volume):

3 parts sand (medium grade)
4 parts ground sphagnum moss
5 parts Canadian peat (screened ¼ inch)

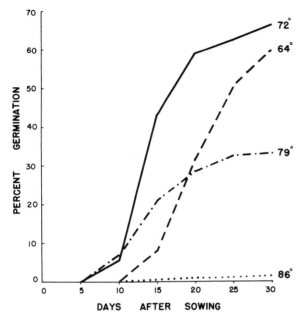

Figure 4–4 Seed germination of mountain laurel at four temperatures: 64, 72, 79, and 86°F. Note particularly the low germination percentage at the two high temperatures. (Jaynes 1971e)

This mix has a pH of about 4.2. By using a medium without soil, one minimizes the danger from soil-borne pathogens, and, in addition, the peat and sphagnum moss contribute some antibiotic activity. The clear plastic boxes measure 3½ by 7 by 1¾ inches high and are placed 9 to 12 inches below fluorescent lights. Use standard flats to germinate larger quantities of seed. In flats, the mix should be modified with coarse builder's sand or perlite to increase drainage.

These and other mixes exhibit an unusual property; when stored they do not support good seed germination and growth. Though difficult to believe, this virtually aseptic, nonsoil mix, stored nearly dry, deteriorates as a germination medium in a few months. I have observed this deterioration of the medium time and again, and one of my colleagues, who uses a quite different medium for germinating gloxinias, has had the same difficulty with his stored mixes. Possibly the natural antibiotic qualities of the sphagnum moss and peat oxidize and deteriorate when mixed with other materials. This could account for the growth of fungi and a marked decrease in germination and initial vigor of seedlings. So I would advise you not to prepare more germination mix than will be used within two months.

As mentioned above, the mix used in the small germination boxes is not entirely satisfactory for seed germination in flats, for in the larger, deeper trays more compaction occurs and less internal drainage and aeration are possible. This deficiency of seedling mixes is common; it causes rapid growth of seedlings around the edge and stagnation in the center of the container. Here is a mix that has worked well for germination of seed in flats:

   1 bu peat
   ½ bu perlite
   ½ bu vermiculite
   ½ bu milled sphagnum
   ½ bu coarse builder's sand
   1 oz hydrated lime

To simplify this mix try it without vermiculite, milled sphagnum, and sand.

After filling the flats, gently firm the surface with a board. Wet the medium thoroughly prior to sowing by setting the flats in a shallow tray of water (you can make one with a sheet of plastic placed on a level surface and bounded by 2-inch-high boards). If you spray the mix directly from above, it may compact and leave a layer of perlite on top. If the surface appears too rough, sprinkle a thin layer of milled sphagnum on it.

The seeds should be sown on the surface of the mix and *not covered.* They need light and will not germinate in the dark. A moist medium and high humidity are necessary to germinate. Once the seed is germinated and well rooted, the surface of the medium should be allowed to dry occasionally to retard algal and moss growth.

It is not necessary to fertilize the mix until true leaves are formed. Then sprinkle on a solution of soluble 15-15-15 fertilizer which has been prepared at the rate of 1 teaspoon per gallon. After the first application, sprinkle more on at two- and three-week intervals, testing the mix from time to time to prevent overfertilizing and to detect a possible imbalance of nutrients or a pH change.

If they do not become too crowded or matted by algae and moss, the seedlings can be left in flats for more than two months. Remember that, once the seeds have germinated and developed roots, the surface of the medium should be allowed to dry every few days. You may use Dithane M-45 (6 ounces per thousand square feet or 1 teaspoon per 13 square feet) to control the algae, but use it sparingly. Heavy applications may injure the seedlings. Should a heavy mat of algae and moss form, it is best to transplant the seedlings, leaving behind as much of the algae and moss as possible.

Most seeds will germinate in ten to twenty-one days. Light intensity should be at least 110 foot-candles (50 μ einsteins/m^2/sec). A bank of four closely spaced standard fluorescent tubes with a white reflector will furnish this much light when placed 9 to 12 inches above the seeds. The bulb length will depend on the area to be covered. When growing the seedlings indoors, I have used sixteen hours of light, from 8 A.M. to midnight. In the greenhouse during the winter I extend the day length with 75-watt floodlights from 10 P.M. to 2 A.M. These incandescent lights are used not to increase growth (by photosynthesis) but to keep the seedlings from becoming dormant. The reflector bulbs are spaced every 4 feet, 30 inches above the plants, so that the plants receive only 8 to 10 foot-candles of artificial light in the middle of the night.

Experiments with mountain laurel and sheep laurel seed demonstrate that germination can be hastened by starting the seeds under an atmosphere enriched with carbon dioxide (CO_2). The benefit of CO_2 on increasing plant growth is well known and is discussed in the next chapter, but its effect on stimulating germination is less well understood. The translucent seed coats of laurel allow the seed leaves to green up, and in the presence of high CO_2 levels their development and growth is speeded up, resulting in faster germination.

Time of Sowing

Seeds from even late-maturing species can be harvested and cleaned by late fall. They should be planted indoors under lights by December 1 so that by spring husky seedlings will have developed, which can be moved outdoors and will continue to thrive throughout the normal growing season.

MYCORRHIZA—FUNGI ASSOCIATED WITH THE ROOTS

Many plants, especially in the Ericaceae, have fungi that are intimately associated with the roots, and are called symbiotic mycorrhiza. These fungi are dependent on the roots, and in turn they may in some way assist the plant in assimilating nutrients and water or in preventing attacks by other fungi. Indeed, *Kalmia* plants have been described as normally having mycorrhizal associates within (endophyte) and outside (ectophyte) the roots. They are not carried in the seed or on any other parts of the plant growing above ground.

A helpful paper by William Flemer of Princeton, New Jersey, deals with isolating these fungi and growing mountain laurel seedlings with and without them. Under sterile conditions he isolated pure cultures of various root-associated fungi and then inoculated the root area of aseptically grown seedlings with them. He observed a positive growth response by the seedlings to the presence of the most commonly isolated endophyte. On the basis of Flemer's work one may conclude that this is an important mycorrhizal association beneficial to the growth of mountain laurel.

I have not repeated Flemer's experiments and take no special measures to inoculate seedlings. In fact, I do not use soil, a possible source of mycorrhizal inoculum, in the germinating mix, because it is also a source of pathogenic fungi. However, the beneficial organism may be present in peat or sphagnum, and the plants may thus become naturally inoculated. It is also possible that mycorrhizal association does not occur and/or is less important to seedling growth in more complex media than in the sterile, defined environment of the laboratory. More research in both laboratory and field is needed to determine the true function of these fungi in seedling growth.

THE SEEDS AND THEIR GERMINATION
Western Laurel, *K. microphylla*; Eastern Bog Laurel, *K. polifolia*; and Sheep Laurel, *K. angustifolia*

These three species are the easiest to germinate, because their seed has no strong dormancy requirement.* Interestingly, these species, with no special pregermination requirements are the ones with

---

* There has been just a hint of partial dormancy in sheep laurel seed from plants of the southern part of the range.

elongated and wing-like seeds (Figures 4–1, 4–2). Dormancy may be related to the tighter, harder-appearing seed shape, but then the relationship may be entirely accidental. The number of seeds per capsule varies from a few up to about 200 in the western laurel and eastern bog laurel and 300 in sheep laurel. The number of seeds per capsule is less when pollination was poor or where there was an excessive number of flowers.

Mountain Laurel, *K. latifolia*

Fresh mountain laurel seed will germinate without any special treatment (Figure 4–5). However, cold stratification for eight weeks or merely soaking the seeds overnight in 200 ppm gibberellin increases germination 50 percent. Seed stored for a year or two will germinate even better than fresh seed, because simple dry storage overcomes the partial dormancy requirement of fresh seed.

Dormancy requirements probably evolved as an adaptation to

Figure 4–5 Flats of mountain laurel seedlings being grown in a commercial greenhouse. Recently sown seeds at left are covered with newspaper to give shade and lessen drying.

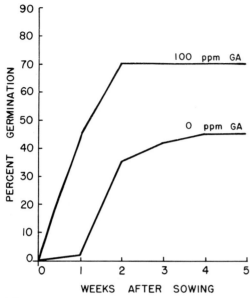

Figure 4–6   Enhancement of germination of mountain laurel seed with gibberellin. Note 45 percent of the untreated seed germinated and about 70 percent of the GA treated seed. As with the white wicky seed, gibberellic acid (GA) substitutes for the longer effect of stratification that occurs in nature. Rates of GA higher than 100 to 200 ppm cause excessive elongation of the seedlings. (Jaynes 1971c)

prevent all the seed from germinating at once in the wild. For example, if there were an extended warm period in the fall after the seed capsules had split, then only the seed without a dormancy requirement would be able to germinate; the rest would remain quiescent during the winter until favorable conditions occurred in the spring.

Treatment of mountain laurel seed is necessary or valuable only when seed is in short supply, as that from controlled crosses, or when the expectation is that germination percentages of fresh seed will be abnormally low. Untreated fresh seed usually has a 20- to 50-percent germination rate in three to four weeks. By treating with gibberellin, germination is greater and a bit faster, and emergence is more uniform (Figure 4–6).

Mountain laurel seed has a ribbed or striated surface. It weighs more than sandhill and white wicky seed, about 1.4 million seeds per ounce. Even seeds from one plant may vary considerably in size, and most capsules contain between 100 and 250 seeds, but some with more than 400 seeds have been observed.

In the wild, mountain laurel seeds germinate on bare mineral soil or on low growing moss. Since the soil cannot be allowed to dry, seedlings are commonly found on north-facing slopes of road cuts with mature plants above: the source of the seed that is dispersed by gravity and wind.

White Wicky, *K. cuneata*

Freshly harvested seed of white wicky has a poor rate of germination, usually less than 5 percent. However, seed treated in a moist-cold environment (stratified) for eight to sixteen weeks shows a ten-fold germination increase. To stratify such fine seed, mix them with a small quantity of moist sand and place them in a refrigerator at a constant temperature of 40°F. Or simply sow the seed on the moistened germination mix, and refrigerate at 40°F. The latter technique works well for small quantities of seed sown in small plastic containers taped shut to prevent evaporation during the cold treatment. Seed harvested in late fall or winter has often been naturally stratified enough to satisfy the dormancy requirement.

A short treatment (12 to 24 hours) with gibberellin, a naturally occurring plant hormone, can be used instead of the stratification procedure. A solution of 500 to 1000 ppm (parts per million) of gibberellin is effective (Figure 4–7). Before sowing the seeds, place them on a piece of filter or blotting paper saturated with the gibberellin solution for twelve to twenty-four hours. The effect on germination is the same as if they had received eight weeks of moist-cold treatment. Since it is difficult to remove the seed from the wet paper immediately after treatment, let the paper and seeds dry. Then the seed simply will roll off the paper and can be handled normally.

The white wicky seed capsules (Figure 4–8) hold as many as 200 seeds; the average is closer to 100. They are so small that approximately 1.7 million seeds would weigh only 1 ounce.

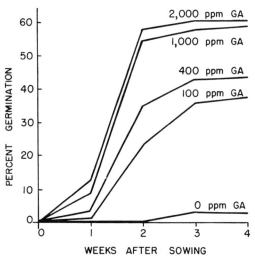

WEEKS AFTER SOWING

Figure 4-7 Gibberellin (GA) breaks the dormancy of white wicky seed. It is a substitute for the effects of stratification that occur in nature during winter. Instead of treating the seed for eight weeks with moist cold, it can be treated for twenty-four hours on blotting paper wetted with a solution of GA to break the dormancy. (Jaynes 1971c)

Figure 4-8 White wicky in late fall after the leaves have dropped. The seed capsules are held by gracefully curved peduncles.

Sandhill Laurel, *K. hirsuta*

This species exhibits the most unusual requirement for germination, and its seed is the most difficult to germinate. The seed is incredibly small; as many as 5 million to the ounce. There are only a few other plants in the world with such minute seeds. Yet because of its roundness, it rolls easily on paper and can be readily separated from the chaff. The difficulty with this seed is in fulfilling the dormancy requirement to insure germination. Seed sown on the usual mix will not germinate for at least four weeks. Germination may continue erratically for three or more months, often with less than 20-percent success.

I have improved success by treating the seed with heat-humidity prior to sowing. Seeds were placed in small open vials set in a closed jar containing ½ inch of water. These jars were then heated in an incubator or constant-temperature water bath. The higher the temperature, the shorter need be the treatment time (Figure 4–9). At the unusually high temperature of 176°F, the seed should be

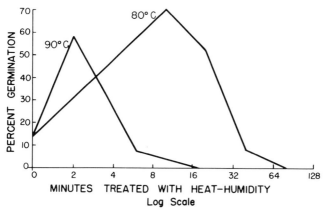

Figure 4–9 Germination of sandhill laurel seed after treatment at near-boiling temperatures (90°C = 194°F and 80°C = 176°F) and high humidity. Even with treatment, seed of sandhill laurel germinates slowly. The data shown were for eleven weeks after sowing. Germination of the other laurel species, by comparison, is usually complete within three to four weeks. (Jaynes 1971c)

treated for 10 to 20 minutes. Yet at 140°F the treatment must continue for about twelve hours. Treatments up to temperatures of 194°F were effective but dangerous, because boiling kills the seeds. Seed treated with a solution of gibberellin (2000 ppm) for forty-eight hours had a positive effect on the germination of both untreated and heat-treated seeds.

This heat-humidity treatment that stimulates *K. hirsuta* seed germination would surely kill seeds of most other plants. During the early stages of these seed germination experiments I corresponded with T. S. Shinn from Leicester, North Carolina, who had been frustrated in his many attempts to germinate sandhill laurel. I explained what we were doing and, using his oven, he treated the seed at about 175°F for twenty minutes. Thus he succeeded in germinating sandhill laurel for the first time. I was delighted to learn that we were not dealing with a mere laboratory effect.

Heat-humidity treatments with sandhill laurel have been performed many times, and, although often successful, they are unfortunately not always effective. Therefore other treatments need to be worked out that will assist us in obtaining maximum, fast, reliable germination with this species. One thing I have noted is that untreated seed, which has a low germination rate in plastic boxes under lights, will often germinate after several weeks on the surface of the same medium when watered regularly in a flat in a greenhouse. Perhaps either the sunlight, the bacterial action, or the leaching effect of the water triggered germination.

This unusual dormancy requirement of sandhill laurel seed could have evolved in the natural environment as a response to recurrent ground fires. During a fire, soil temperatures in the upper ¼ inch often reach 170°F. Humidity and vapor pressure in the top layer of soil increase as the fire passes, because water vapor is forced downward from the burning litter and condenses there, like vapor in an inverted still. A seed adapted to germinate after a fire would find itself on a seedbed of bare mineral soil. It would be relatively free of competition, since the fire would destroy seeds of most other plants on or near the soil surface. Yet, after a ground fire, shade from large shrubs and especially trees would frequently be present.

Fire is accepted in the southeastern coastal plain as a natural part of the environment. Other plants in the area are adapted to fire, although often not in the same way. Longleaf pine, for example, will lose its competitive advantage unless there are occasional ground fires which kill many plants but not the young pine seedlings or large pine trees. Giant sequoias with their fire-resistant bark would also be at a disadvantage without occasional ground fires to destroy competition. Lodgepole, jack, and other pines depend on the heat of fires to open their cones for seed release.

The unique dormancy requirement of sandhill laurel seed may have been a key factor in the spread of *Kalmia* onto the coastal plain. If this is true, then the Cuban laurel, *K. ericoides*, which represents a further extension of the genus, might have a similar seed dormancy requirement.

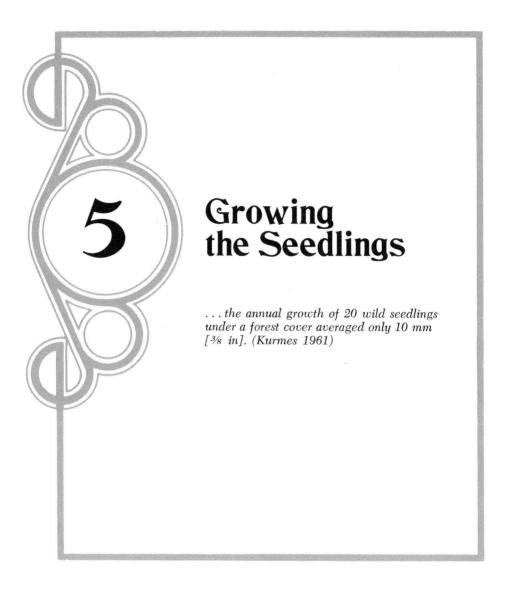

5

Growing the Seedlings

... the annual growth of 20 wild seedlings under a forest cover averaged only 10 mm [³/₈ in]. (Kurmes 1961)

With laurel, especially mountain laurel, the time from sowing to flowering may seem interminable. We are always on the lookout for any techniques to speed growth of the seedlings and to bring about early flower bud formation.

MEDIUM AND SPACING

To insure the best growth, seedlings should be transplanted two to six months after germination. However, nurseries commonly leave

55

their plants in the flats for a full year after germination; this probably adds an additional year to the time until flowering. If the seed is sown in late fall, the seedlings should be ready for transplanting in midwinter. I generally prick them off with forceps when they have one to three true leaves and space them 2 inches apart in a flat. I use a dibble board the size of the flat with sixty nails equally spaced to mark the position for planting each seedling. The choice of mix varies from grower to grower; I like the following for small transplants:

1 bu peat
½ bu perlite
¼ bu vermiculite
¼ bu milled sphagnum
1 oz hydrated lime
2 tsp 15-15-15 soluble fertilizer watered-in

To simplify the mix, try it without vermiculite and milled sphagnum. The lime adds calcium and raises the pH of the mix, and the hydrated lime is more active and faster acting than regular limestone. When using limestone, use one-third more material than for hydrated lime.

OPERATION HEADSTART—FERTILIZING THE AIR

Enrichment of the atmosphere around seedlings with carbon dioxide (CO_2) is an economical means of achieving a dramatic increase in plant size. Carbon dioxide is an essential raw material for plant growth, and its low concentration is often the critical factor limiting growth. Normal air contains about 300 ppm CO_2, but some plants may use up to ten times that amount. An increase in laurel seed germination and a large increase in seedling size were achieved by exposing the sown seeds for seven weeks to an atmosphere of 2000 ppm CO_2 (Figure 5–1).

An increased concentration of carbon dioxide alone will not stimulate plant growth. Other conditions, such as light, nutrients, or temperature must be equally favorable. We found that 600 foot-candles (250 μ einsteins/m^2 sec at 400 to 700 nm) were needed for good growth with CO_2 enrichment. This was attained in the laboratory with high-output fluorescent tubes and in the greenhouse by

 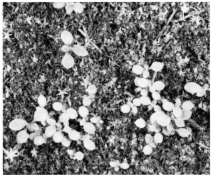

Figure 5–1 Mountain laurel seedlings seven weeks from sowing. The plants on the left were exposed to normal air and most have only one true leaf, whereas the plants on the right, exposed to 2000 ppm CO_2, are much larger and many have four true leaves (white line is 0.4 inch or 1 cm).

supplementing natural daylight in winter with fluorescent light to extend day length and to supplement daylight on cloudy days. Somewhat lower light intensities were adequate in normal air, but of course growth was less. Low light intensity produces spindly seedlings.

Greenhouse operators have used enriched CO_2 atmospheres for many years, and therefore several techniques are known for increasing the CO_2 concentration. Large greenhouses use CO_2 generators that burn propane gas; greenhouses smaller than 20 by 50 feet use one of three methods: dry ice, compressed gas, or combustion (Mastalerz 1969). Each has its advantages and disadvantages. The source of the CO_2 makes no difference to the plants, unless, of course, it contains toxic impurities, something not likely with these methods. Plants themselves give off CO_2 at night or on dark, overcast days and utilize the enriched atmosphere only on bright or sunny days. The CO_2 source therefore need only operate during the day and only on days when the greenhouse vents are closed most of the time. Generally winter is the most practical time to add CO_2 to the growing atmosphere.

The most advantageous time to expose laurel to an enriched CO_2 atmosphere is from seed germination until after several true leaves are formed—that is, from December until March. Many seedlings can be handled in a relatively small space, and the rapid increase in plant size in the first few months is of utmost importance in reducing the time until the plants reach flowering age. Obtaining a 3-inch plant from seed outdoors under natural conditions takes two to three years, whereas this can be achieved during one winter and spring under controlled greenhouse conditions. With a winter headstart the young seedlings are already "one-year-size" or more in May and are ready to take advantage of the full growing season outdoors.

Dry Ice

Dry ice is CO_2 in the solid state. It is more expensive than other forms, but it is pure and relatively easy to handle. For example, it can be stored in a home freezer. The daily requirement for each 100 square feet of greenhouse floor space is about 1¾ pounds. To obtain even distribution, place the required amount in equal portions on the walkway three or four times during the day, or use an open insulated box which allows slower evaporation and requires only a single placement in the morning.

Compressed Gas in Cylinders

Carbon dioxide may also be purchased as a compressed gas in cylinders. The gas itself is relatively inexpensive, but the required flow meter, pressure regulator, solenoid valve, and time clock add up to a considerable initial expense (Figure 5–2). The system is usually regulated by a time clock which opens the valve shortly after sunrise and closes it an hour before sunset. Large cylinders contain 60 pounds of CO_2 or about 522 cubic feet. A flow rate of 1½ to 2 cubic feet of CO_2 per hour per 100 square feet of greenhouse will give about 2000 ppm CO_2. If CO_2 is fed for nine hours a day at this rate to an area of 100 square feet, then a large cylinder will last four to six weeks.

Alcohol Burning

The least expensive and perhaps simplest means of supplying CO_2 is to burn methyl or ethyl alcohol. To obtain 2000 ppm CO_2 per 100 square feet of greenhouse space, 2 to 3 fluid ounces of ethanol or

Figure 5-2 Experimental equipment for passing CO_2-enriched air over germinating seedlings: air pump, CO_2 tank, mixing valve, flow meters, and plastic chambers containing seed flats.

3 to 4 fluid ounces of methanol must be burned per nine-hour day. To lessen the danger of fire, a kerosene lantern or similar device is used to enclose the alcohol flame. A small alcohol lamp with a ¼-inch-diameter wick and low flame burns about 1 ounce of alcohol in nine hours. One disadvantage of the combustion method is the production of heat and water vapor. Neither is a serious problem, unless the heat necessitates increased ventilation which would disperse the CO_2. In large greenhouses it is practical to partition off, with clear plastic curtains, the area where CO_2 enrichment is desired.

The actual concentrations of CO_2 achieved with any one of the preceding methods will vary somewhat depending on the height and tightness of the greenhouse. Anything between 400 and 3000 ppm will help the plants. If the 2000 ppm is maintained, you should have no qualms about working in the enriched atmosphere.

Most laboratory devices for measuring CO_2 concentration are expensive and cumbersome. However, the Kitagawa gas detector distributed by Bendix is a moderately priced sampler adequate for greenhouses. Growers of large numbers of plants should consider it.

Carbon dioxide provides only one of the needs of growing plants. The others should not be neglected, especially in the enriched atmosphere. In fact, when the CO_2 concentration is increased, plants are able to utilize more light and nutrients. So take full advantage of the enriched atmosphere by paying careful attention to supplying sufficient light, maintaining the right temperature, and adding adequate nutrients and water. With careful management one enjoys substantially larger grown plants in much less time.

Despite attempts to provide the proper environment, growth of mountain laurel seedlings may stagnate a month or two after germination. Arie Radder of Imperial Nurseries has found that such seedlings can be stimulated to elongate and grow by spraying them once or twice with a 200 ppm water solution of gibberellic acid.

GROWING IN CONTAINERS

For the nurseryman the ideal way to maintain optimal growth once plants are well started is to grow them in containers. These are easier to plant: digging and burlapping are eliminated and the mechanics of the operation become almost independent of weather. In addition, more plants can be grown per acre. However, mass growing of plants in containers is relatively new and certainly in its infancy for laurel. So for every nurseryman who has been successful with mountain laurel in containers, one finds two who have had problems. The requirements in general are the same as for other ericaceous plants with only slight modifications in media, fertilizer and watering. The medium must be well drained and have an acid pH. Nutrients must be available but not in high concentration. The problem of yellowing of the last flush of growth in the early fall is common and can be lessened, if not eliminated, by maintaining good aeration, adding chelated iron (e.g., Sequestrene), and keeping a good balance between available nitrogen and potassium.

There is little experience with a proper container media for laurel; the opinions that do exist are not in agreement. The work of Dr. Henry DeRoo of the Connecticut Agricultural Experiment Station confirms the need for good drainage and aeration. This statement is so often repeated in horticultural literature that it has lost its impact, but growers of mountain laurel had best heed it. DeRoo found that the standard container media for growing ericaceous material in two large nursery firms caused chlorotic mountain laurel plants within two months. The basic ingredients of these mixes were: (A) 2 parts Canadian peat, 2 parts native peat (muck), 1 part sand, and 1 part perlite; and (B) 1 part native peat and 1 part sand. Interestingly, rhododendrons and azaleas grew better in these mixes than did laurel. A third commercial medium, to which the plants responded much more favorably, was: (C) 1 part Canadian peat, 1 part sand, and 2 parts bark (mixed hardwood); the bark assured good drainage. The experimental mix that proved best of all was: (D) 2 parts Canadian peat, 1 part sand, and 1 part bark.

Additional nutrients were added to this mix as follows: 2 pounds dolomitic limestone, 3 pounds gypsum (landplaster), 2½ pounds 20-percent superphosphate, 1½ pounds ureaform, 1 ounce New Iron, and 2 ounces trace elements each to the cubic yard. All the mixes in the experiment had a pH of 5.0 to 5.5 and were fertilized weekly according to need as determined by a soil test. A mix, intermediate to C and D, having equal parts of peat, sand, and bark seems also satisfactory.

A mix I have used with good success is one containing equal parts of Canadian peat, coarse perlite, and silty loam high in organic matter. But the drawback to any medium containing soil is the difficulty in obtaining soil of the same quality from year to year. Because soil so often varies, it is perhaps best avoided in commercial production.

The need for fertilization depends on the medium and local growing conditions. So once the needs are determined, then nutrients can be supplied through the irrigation water, applied on top of the medium, or mixed in the media at the time of potting. Slow-release fertilizers such as Osmocote (14-14-14) last longer and require less frequent application. Laurel is not a "heavy feeder"; hence apply less, perhaps one-fourth the label-recommended application which is generally based on heavier-feeding, faster-growing plants. The soil should be tested regularly and the pH should be kept at about 4.8 to 5.5.

So follow these methods (Table 5–1) and you will have handsome, budded plants in three years: one winter inside and three growing seasons outdoors (Figures 5–3, 5–4, 5–5, 5–6).

Table 5–1 Schedule from Sowing to Flowering

I. Indoors—greenhouse or bank of lights needed

   A. Sow by December 1 (at least 150 foot-candles of light and a temperature of 70 to 75° required).

   B. Enrich with CO_2 within two weeks (light intensity of 500 to 2000 foot-candles suggested).

   C. Transplant seedlings after eight weeks (by February 1).

   D. Maintain enriched CO_2 for another four to eight weeks.

   E. Transplant seedlings (should be 1 to 2 inches high) June 1 to:

      1. lath house or protected bed;

      2. or place in 1- to 2-quart containers.

   F. 1. After two years in lath house transplant in early spring to field.

      2. Overwinter containers in unheated, plastic-film-covered shelters and transplant to larger containers in spring if necessary.

   G. Leave until budded and then transplant to permanent location or sell. Time span for mountain laurel from seed to budded plants should be three to five years, depending on how well optimum conditions were maintained.

II. Outdoors

   A. Sow in early spring on bare, mineral soil, shaded to prevent the surface from drying, or sow on mix in flats.

   B. Cover seedlings with straw or conifer branches in late fall or protect flats of seedlings in cold frame.

   C. Transplant from seed bed or flats and space out in protected beds.

   D. When 4 to 6 inches high, transplant (early spring) to field or containers.

Figure 5–3 Seedling mountain laurel in 8-inch can at the end of the third year.

Figure 5–4 Red-bud mountain laurel propagated from cuttings and growing in Oregon.

Figure 5–5 Temporary structures for overwintering evergreen plants, grown in containers at Baker Nursery, West Suffield, Connecticut. These are pipe hoop houses covered with plastic sheeting that is put on in October and removed in May. Plants can be shipped any time during the year, and winter burn of foliage is virtually eliminated.

Figure 5–6 Mountain laurel seedlings just after starting their third year's growth, transplanted in early spring and mulched with wood chips. To aid in weed control, granular simazine was applied at a rate of 3 pounds active material per acre with a cyclone spreader after a few heavy rains had settled the soil and plants.

GROWTH REGULATORS

Many growth regulators which improve habit or increase flowering are used in the commercial production of ornamental plants. Little is known about the effect of these compounds on the laurels. At least the more promising ones should be tested on mountain laurel because of their potential value.

Off-Shoot-O, a chemical pinching agent, has been used successfully to "prune" the tips of azaleas. This or a similar compound might be useful in preventing legginess in mountain laurel. Other growth retardants are capable of limiting vegetative growth and stimulating flower bud production. These would be particularly useful with plants that have been pushed hard for several years to obtain maximum size.

We had some success with Phosphon and CCC (Cyocel), growth retardants, when applied to mountain laurel seedlings in their third year of growth. The experiments were conducted using plants in containers and also in the field. Although more tests are needed, the following observations and tentative conclusions appear valid:

1. Phosphon at rates between 0.4 and 0.8 grams per plant are effective in stimulating flower bud formation on seedlings in containers and in the field.

2. Combinations of Phosphon and CCC (0.4 to 0.6 grams and 0.3 grams, respectively, per plant) also were promising. Higher rates of CCC caused discoloration or injury to the leaves.

3. We observed a dramatic difference in response depending on the pedigree (genotype) of three-year-old plants. Seedlings of some crosses produced no flowers regardless of treatment, whereas seedlings of the same size from different parents were quite responsive. As with other kinds of plants, a certain minimum size has to be reached before flowering can be induced and that is dependent on genetic makeup. The three-year plants had reached what is the critical size for laurel, 8 to 10 inches in height.

Vegetative Propagation

In the woods its ... shoots extend laterally to take advantage of the side light and are often bent down by the dead leaves and branches falling from the tree tops. Where the snow lies deep, it tends further to weight them down, until finally many of them lie in contact with the ground. Dead leaves and litter soon cover them and after a few years, when the debris has rotted and become part of the soil, they take root and give rise to new shoots. Where the contact with the parent is broken new plants are formed. This is the process of natural layering. Often, however, the contact is not broken, and thus the soil becomes filled with a dense, widely ramified set of laurel roots, and the surface becomes covered with a tangled mass of branches to the height of a man's knees. This tangled mass excludes almost all other vegetation from under the trees. (Buttrick 1924)

PROPAGATION BY CUTTINGS

One of the most satisfactory means of multiplying selected cultivars is to root branch cuttings. This popular method is used with rhododendrons, azaleas, and other ericaceous plants. Some laurel species root readily, but, unfortunately, mountain laurel is the most intransigent of all in this regard. It can be done, though, and refinements in technique promise continued improvement. The situation is perhaps similar to that faced by rhododrendon propagators twenty years ago. Of the many cultivars available, only a few responded to the commonly used techniques. Adaptation and more sophisticated use of auxins, mist, plastic tents, plus improvement of stock, have greatly increased our ability to mass-produce rhododendron cultivars from cuttings. Some of these same techniques are applicable to mountain laurel, and progress will continue as increasing efforts are devoted to this species.

Facilities, Media, Temperature

Cuttings are most often rooted in a greenhouse, although a small "cold" frame with heating cables will do, and even an indoor case, where plants depend entirely on artificial light, can be used. Since cuttings obviously have no roots to absorb water, they must be exposed to high humidity. Most commonly this is supplied as mist over the cuttings or by enclosing the propagation bench with clear plastic film to form a humid chamber.

MIST PROPAGATION   The successful operation of an intermittent mist system depends on a good supply of nonalkaline water. Low-volume atomizing nozzles spaced 1 to 2 feet above the cutting bench insure good coverage of the cuttings. An electric valve (solenoid) can be regulated by any one of the available devices which control the mist and keep the foliage moist, yet do not allow the medium to become soggy. Electric time clocks, electronic leaves, and evaporative pans can be used to regulate the cycling of the mist. The most satisfactory controls have a photocell* which make the amount of mist dependent on the amount of light available. Thus when a cloud passes, the control immediately compensates by calling for less mist. Time clocks are insensitive to light and weather conditions; electronic leaves salt up; evaporative pans tend to stick or are too readily affected by air currents. The one disadvantage of a photocell control is the initial expense; but if it prevents even one failure, it more than pays for itself. When a mist system must be left unattended for a few days, the photocell control is the most reliable. Whatever control device is used, you must determine the correct amount of mist by observation and testing. On a sunny day a

---

* Solatrol available from General Scientific Supply, Sherman Avenue, Hamden, Connecticut.

common requirement would be five seconds of mist every three minutes.

Mist applications are especially valuable with soft or semihard cuttings in the summer when outside temperatures are high. Mist has the inherent disadvantage of causing leaching, which especially affects slow rooting material. After two to three months in mist, un-rooted cuttings tend to get "hard"; yet in a plastic tent we have succeeded in keeping mountain laurel cuttings in good condition for as long as two years with some rooting occurring throughout the entire period.

PLASTIC TENT   One of the easiest and most reliable means of pro-viding high humidity for cuttings is to cover the bench with a light frame of 1- by 2-inch boards or turkey wire and to cover this with 4-mil clear polyethylene (Figure 6–1). The edges of the plastic should be tucked on the inside of the bench to allow condensation on the inside of the plastic to drip back into the medium. This is

Figure 6–1   Plastic tents for rooting laurel cuttings. Heating pipes are under the bench, and the plastic side curtain traps the hot air and forces heat up through bench and rooting medium. Shade placed over tent prevents overheating on sunny days.

essentially a closed system with only drain holes under the bench to allow for the exchange of air and the loss of excessive moisture. Such a "sweat box" requires little care. Once cuttings are stuck, watered in, and the tent closed, no further care is needed for about four weeks. At that time the medium should be checked to see if additional water is needed. If the mix, bench, and cuttings were clean at the start, then fungal pathogens should be no problem.

It is important to monitor the temperature, especially on sunny days. If the temperature goes above 90°F, then additional shading is necessary. The trick with a tent is to get as much daylight as possible without overheating. So of course adequate shading in November is inadequate in June.

MEDIA   As with other aspects of propagation, there is no concensus on the best medium to root cuttings. One commonly used for rhododendrons is also good for laurel: 2 parts fibrous, sphagnum peat moss to 1 part coarse perlite. The ratio may be altered to equal parts of each. Many propagators used to insist on fibrous German peat, but its scarcity has led to the substitution of Canadian peat, which has proved satisfactory. The peat moss–perlite mix provides an acid, light, porous medium of high water-holding capacity. Normally the medium should be spread 6 to eight inches deep in the bench. Do not use the mix for successive batches of cuttings; this often leads to problems with pathogens and a decrease in rooting.

TEMPERATURE   Between 70 and 80°F is the best temperature for root formation and growth. In summer the problem is trying to hold the temperature down to this level, and in winter the problem is to maintain this temperature. Do not assume the rooting medium is the same as the air temperature. In an open bench the mix will be from 5 to 10° *cooler* than the air temperature. Two ways to make sure that the medium remains at the required temperature is to install electric heating cables and a thermostat in the mix itself. The other way is to direct greenhouse heat under the propagation benches and to trap it there by using side curtains of plastic or felt paper. In this way the heat radiates up through the rooting medium. As long as the medium is 70 to 75°, it really does not matter if the air temperature is considerably lower. In fact, if foliage is kept cool until roots are formed, the cuttings will more readily flush into growth when the air temperature is later raised.

PREPARATION OF CUTTINGS   Summer cuttings should be taken while they are turgid; therefore, do not collect any past midmorning on sunny days. In the fall or winter, collection time of day is less important. Cuttings which are not immediately stuck in the bench can be stored in the refrigerator at 40°F for a few days in the summer and for a few weeks in the fall or winter.

One of the mysteries of plant propagation is that some obviously mistreated cuttings do root, whereas some coddled ones do not. Nurserymen tell of cuttings forgotten in the trunk of the car or under the work bench for a few days that surprisingly root when finally stuck in the bench. On occasion I have been amazed and delighted to root cuttings of mountain laurel that were badly mauled and delayed in transit. And so the mystery remains regarding the proper pretreatment of cuttings.

Wounding of cuttings is commonly practiced with rhododendrons and may be of benefit with mountain laurel, but with the other laurel species it is not worth the extra effort. To wound the cutting, remove a sliver of bark with a bit of wood from either side of the cutting. Each cut should be about 1 inch long if made above the base, or 1½ inches long if it extends to the base.

Some propagators routinely rinse their cuttings in a water bath containing a fungicide, insecticide, and/or antidesiccant. Hobbyists can safely skip the additives and just rinse the cuttings in cool water. However, a clean bench and a clean mix are essential. Several days before the benches are to be filled, all traces of the old mix should be removed; the benches should be rinsed with water, doused with a nonresidual disinfectant like sodium hypochlorite (Clorox), and allowed to dry.

LIGHTS   Extend the daylight period to sixteen hours during the short days of fall and early winter, because long days benefit rooting and subsequent growth. In practice, the day length can be extended by having lights come on at dusk for a few hours. The same effect is achieved more economically by having the lights come on for less time in the middle of the night. Physiologists, working with other plants, have found that it is the length of the *dark* period that is critical; hence, light in the middle of the night more efficiently breaks the period of continuous darkness. One 75-watt incandescent reflector floodlight for every 12 square feet of bench space should be adequate if placed 30 inches above the plants.

Western Laurel, *K. microphylla,* and Eastern Bog Laurel, *K. polifolia*

Unlike most laurels, the soft or semihard cuttings of these species are easy to root (Figure 6–2). No special cut, wound, or leaf removal is necessary. Cuttings need be only 1 to 2 inches long. They can be handled in a tent or under mist, and with no auxin treatment roots will appear within three weeks. Under lights and warm (70 to 75°) conditions, they will continue to grow. The young plants may require pinching to encourage good habit and these pinched shoots make excellent cuttings.

Figure 6–2 Cuttings of bog laurel after three weeks in a plastic tent. In four more weeks these plants could be cut back to obtain more cuttings for propagation and to force branching.

Mountain Laurel, *K. latifolia*

Few horticulturists agree on when is the best time for cuttings, whether or not wounding is beneficial, which media to use, or even how long rooting will take. As an example, investigators have reported January, March, June and July, and August to December as the "best" times to take cuttings.

Lewis Lipp, former horticulturist at Holden Arboretum, recommends taking 2- to 3-inch cuttings of current season's growth from the tips of branches in early August. He suggests that the cut ends be treated with 1% IBA (3-indole butyric acid) in talc before placing them in a plastic-covered tent.

Perhaps it is best to report the results of my own experiments. For me the plastic tent works better than mist for mountain laurel, in large part because of the length of time necessary for rooting. Mist has its greatest value for soft or semihard cuttings taken in the summer when temperatures are high. Its cooling effect is extremely beneficial. This same cooling effect in the fall and winter tends to drop the medium temperature below 70°F and thus delays rooting.

I have had best success with cuttings taken in October, just before a hard freeze; yet cuttings taken from mid-September through November performed nearly as well. Make cuttings about 3 inches long from a single flush of current season growth but not necesarily the last flush. I have not been able to demonstrate a positive response to a number of auxins, fungicides, and other materials which reportedly aid rooting in other ericaceous plants. A five-second dip in an ethyl alcohol solution of 5000 ppm each of NAA (2-naphthalene acetic acid) and IBA is beneficial with some clones. A commercial preparation of this material, called Jiffy Grow, is available from nursery supply houses. One of the difficulties in evaluating these auxins is that different clones appear to respond differently to the same auxin treatment.

Alfred Fordham, propagator at Arnold Arboretum, has had success rooting softwood cuttings that were forced into growth in the winter. A note in an old gardening magazine indicates that a nursery in New York, as long ago as 1893 (Trumpy), was rooting cuttings from young wood of plants grown indoors. The rooting of cuttings from forced plants has worked extremely well with Exbury azaleas and has several advantages. The technique is particularly suitable for container-grown stock plants. Stock plants are allowed to go into their usual fall dormancy and are exposed to cold until mid-January, when they are heated and forced into growth. The new shoots can then be handled under mist or, better, under plastic, with these advantages:

1. Cuttings root more readily.
2. Unlike the rooted fall cutting, the requirement for a cold treatment has been fulfilled.
3. Once rooted, they have a full, normal growing season ahead.

However, despite the promise of this method, my attempts to root cuttings of mountain laurel from plants forced into growth in February and March have been unsuccessful.

STOCK PLANT AGE   One important and often overlooked aspect in rooting mountain laurel and other difficult-to-root plants is the age of the stock. It has been known for years that cuttings from young plants generally root more readily than those from older plants. The classic example is the difference in the rooting ability of "juvenile" and "mature" English ivy (*Hedera helix*). The juvenile vines form roots readily, but the mature, shrub-like form is difficult to root.

Several years of experiments have demonstrated that the same is true in rooting mountain laurel cuttings. Indeed, the percentage of rooted cuttings of one-year-old seedlings, receiving no auxin treatment was 90 percent; the rate of rooting dropped off rapidly with older plants, diminishing to 20 percent for flowering plants. In addition, the speed of formation and quantity of roots on a cutting are greater from young seedlings, and such cuttings will flush into growth more rapidly than cuttings from older plants. Cuttings from flowering plants have the disconcerting tendency to produce flower buds in the propagation bench; these flower buds occupy the sites where vegetative growth should occur.

Cuttings from rooted cuttings and cuttings from young grafts also root more readily than cuttings from the original stock plant. Data given in Table 6–1 show this effect rather dramatically for a red-bud clone. Cuttings taken from cuttings rooted the previous year rooted much better than cuttings from flowering plants of the same clone, 94-percent versus 30-percent.

Clones vary in their ability for cuttings to form roots. Select

Table 6–1 Comparative rooting of cuttings of one clone (137) of mountain laurel taken from stock plants of different ages. No auxin or fungicide treatment.

Age of stock plant	Number of cuttings	Number rooted, Oct. to Feb.	Percent rooted
15-year-old original plant	10	3	30
8-year-old plants from rooted cuttings	16	5	31
1-year-old plants from rooted cuttings	34	32	94

clones that root more readily and then continue to take cuttings from recent propagations, rather than the original or other flowering plants.

An example of a clone that roots readily is our pink selection, 'Pink Surprise', which has consistently rooted 80 percent or better from fall cuttings for six consecutive years. Once rooted plants are obtained, cuttings should be taken from these and not the original plant to maintain as much juvenility as possible. Cuttings can be taken if necessary from one- to two-year-old seedlings if the seedlings are of known pedigree and flower color.

Cuttings, especially those from older plants, may show a reluctance to flush into growth after rooting. If possible, give such cuttings a cold period, 35 to 50° for six weeks, with no artificial light to extend day length. For cuttings taken in October, try this dormancy treatment during February and March. Then in April, when the rooted cuttings are warmed, they should burst into growth. When it was not possible to cool the greenhouse because of the other plants, I have moved flats of rooted cuttings into a dirt cellar where they received eight hours of incandescent light daily. After six to eight weeks of this "winterization," they were brought back into the greenhouse to resume growth.

By carefully selecting and manipulating the stock and then treating the cuttings properly, you will succeed in rooting this difficult species. It does take patience and perseverence.

Sheep Laurel, *K. angustifolia*

Sheep laurel is somewhat easier to root than mountain laurel. Soft-wood cuttings taken during the summer can be rooted, but firmer cuttings taken in late summer and fall are easier to handle and to root. Treat them with the same five-second auxin dip as mountain laurel cuttings.

Whenever possible, choose cuttings without flower buds. They are easier to root and they flush into growth more readily. Cuttings should be 2 to 3 inches long and have two leaf whorls. You need not bother to strip off the lower leaves, or at least not more than one whorl. Newly rooted cuttings will begin growth without first receiving a cool rest period.

White Wicky, *K. cuneata*, and Sandhill Laurel, *K. hirsuta*

My experience in rooting these two undomesticated species is limited, but I do know that greenwood cuttings and semihard cuttings taken in late summer or early fall will root. The auxin treatment is beneficial. Cuttings of white wicky taken too late in the fall will lose their leaves. Extension of the day length with lights in late summer and fall will extend the rooting and growing period. As with mountain laurel, use juvenile wood when possible.

PROPAGATION BY GRAFTING

Outstanding specimens of mountain laurel, which are inordinately difficult to root, are candidates for grafting. Mountain laurel can be grafted with little difficulty, and suckering of the stock is not a serious problem on established grafts. Late winter or early spring is the normal grafting time. Stocks should be replaced in pots or flats in the fall and then exposed to cold temperatures until about the first of February, when they can be warmed up and forced into growth. Vigorous seedlings 4 to 8 inches tall make good stocks, but they should not be grafted until clear signs of root activity are observed by tipping the plant out of the container and looking for new white rootlets on the surface of the root ball. This should occur three weeks after they are given heat.

Dormant scions should be either cleft-grafted or side-veneer-grafted onto the stock as low as possible (Figures 6–3, 6–4). Wrap the graft firmly but not tightly with a rubber band or a rubber budding strip. The grafted plants need to be kept under humid conditions until new cells knit the stock and scion together. A plastic tent makes for the easiest and best environment. After four to six weeks, the tent can be gradually ventilated for a week or two for the plants to adjust to the less humid growing conditions of the greenhouse. When there is no longer any danger of frost, plant the grafts outdoors. You can create individual humid chambers merely by enclosing each potted grafted plant in a plastic bag. An advantage of late winter and early spring grafting is that the grafts put out one flush of growth before the normal growing season even begins.

June grafting can be successful and is most valuable for propagating new selections identified in flower or in cases where it may be inconvenient or impossible to obtain scions the next winter. For June grafting use scions of the current season's growth, firm but not woody. Stocks should be chosen from small plants which grew vigorously the previous year.

Side-veneer or cleft-graft scions onto last year's growth on the smooth part of the stem with few leaves. Tie the unions with cut rubber bands, and handle the grafts the same as in early spring grafting. Approximately seven weeks after grafting, the plants can be set outside in shaded beds. Since June-grafted clones often do not put out a flush of growth until the following spring, the only advantage over grafting the same plants next spring is to serve necessity or convenience.

One rooting method used with difficult-to-root rhododendrons and certain other plants is first to graft the difficult-to-root scion onto a stem section of an easy-to-root selection. Then treat the graft like a cutting, and place the union below the medium surface in the propagation bed. The easy-to-root "stock" will form roots while the graft knits, and months later the scion itself roots. With some combinations a delayed incompatibility will cause the graft union to fail eventually, but not until after the scion roots. It is a promising approach that I tested by grafting mountain laurel selections onto eastern bog laurel and sheep laurel. Several of the grafts on sections of underground stems of sheep laurel were successful, but on the whole the method is unreliable and impractical.

Figure 6–3 A cleft-grafted mountain laurel wrapped with a rubber band. The union should be made as close to the ground as possible. This one is higher than necessary or desirable.

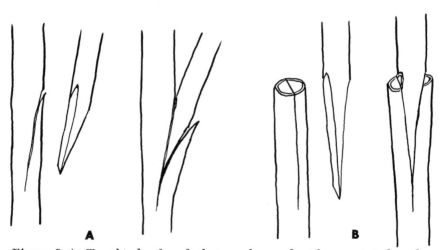

A

B

Figure 6–4 Two kinds of graft that can be used with mountain laurel: (A) side veneer graft, (B) cleft graft. A sharp knife to make smooth cuts, and good matching of the cut surfaces are essential.

PROPAGATION BY LAYERING

Laurels spread and propagate in the wild by natural layering. Bent-over branches become covered with leaf litter and humus, eventually rooting along the portion covered and in contact with the soil. All species will layer, but, since mountain laurel is the slowest to respond, let us look at it first. Heavy snows or other woodland phenomena bend the branches of mountain laurel down so that layering occurs. If the process happens repeatedly for many years, small thickets arise which have their origin in a single plant. I have observed clumps of banded mountain laurel, readily identified by their unique flowers, that measured nearly 20 feet edge to edge, and it is easy to imagine a single plant spreading over an even larger area.

To layer a selection of your own, remove an inch or so of soil beneath a low-lying stem and then bend it to the ground (Figure 6–5). Rooting can be facilitated by girdling: Firmly bind the stem where it comes into contact with the soil with one or more loops of

Figure 6–5   Layering. A lateral branch is placed and pegged into a depression dug alongside the plant. The branch is wounded, covered with a mix of peat moss and soil, and kept moist. After rooting (six to eighteen months for mountain laurel), the layer is cut from the mother plant and transplanted. The number of layers per stock plant is determined by the number of branches that can be pulled to the ground.

wire; bend the stem to break it partially; or make several shallow, encircling knife cuts. Then peg the stem down and cover it with leaf mold or peat moss and soil. Finally, water and mulch. Do not allow the layer to dry out. If started in the spring, roots may have formed by fall, but a second growing season is often necessary for good rooting. Once roots have formed, sever the layer from the mother plant and move it to a protected location. If the roots are not strong, prune back the top when you transplant it to lessen the stress on the transplant.

Layering is a laborious and slow method, yet one that fascinates many gardeners, To propagate just a few plants the technique is as practical as any; however, it has little or no appeal for the nursery-man who needs a more efficient method.

7

Fundamentals of Garden Care

A soil of a peaty nature is best, but in gardens consisting of pure loam they may be grown well by trenching deeply and mixing plenty of well-decayed leaf-soil and as much peat as can be afforded with the top spit [the depth of a blade of a spade]. They can have the same antipathy to lime at the roots, which renders the cultivation of so many ericaceous plants in chalky soils a difficult and expensive matter. A cool and continuously moist soil is an important desideratum, and this is why deep trenching is recommended. In hot, sandy soils the ground should be removed to a depth of 2 feet and placed at the bottom with the best of the natural soil mixed with a heavier loam, filling the upper part with a mixture of peat, leaf-soil, and loam. This may be a troublesome and perhaps costly business, but it is cheapest in the end, and saves much labour in watering during the hot summer weather. (Bean 1897)

It is discouraging to purchase, or be given, a valuable plant only to have it decline and die in the garden. But anyone who has enjoyed success with azaleas and other ericaceous plants should have little trouble with laurel. Their requirements are, in fact, similar.

An initial consideration is whether the plant will be hardy. This can be determined by knowing where the species normally grows and how other specimens have done in your area. Locally grown plants have the advantage of having been exposed and acclimated to the local environment. Species like mountain laurel with extensive north and south range may vary greatly in their hardiness. Plants from the southern end of the range are not adapted to the shorter growing season in the north and will not adapt to it.

Most of us are limited in our choices of planting sites, so we must survey the conditions around our homes carefully before selecting a planting location. None of the laurels will thrive in an exposed location where the soil is left bare and the ground freezes deep in winter or where there is no snow protection; but with protection against winds, all do well in full sunlight. In fact, the more sun they receive, the more dense their growth and the more prolific their flowering. On the other hand, partial shade, as obtained from an overstory of widely spaced trees, is beneficial in prolonging the life of the flowers and extending the blooming period, especially with mountain laurel. Shade becomes even more important with mountain laurel in the mid to southern part of its range where the summer sun is particularly intense (Figures 7–1, 7–2).

Figure 7–1 Mountain laurel, instead of a lawn to mow, is used as a ground cover. House faces south. The low ground cover overhanging the stone wall is bearberry.

Figure 7-2 Naturalized mountain laurel planted at the edge of a lawn.

Avoid low, open areas that constitute potential frost pockets as sites for mountain laurel. This species, adapted to high country, is susceptible to frost injury when planted in low pockets, but the other laurels are more resistant as would be expected from their natural habitat which includes low, wet areas. On clear nights heat is radiated to the open sky from the ground, plants, and air. If there is no breeze, the cold air settles and moves downslope where it collects in depressions, valley bottoms, and along streams, or so-called frost pockets. A change of just a few feet in height may mean a difference of several degrees in minimum temperature. Because a canopy of trees, even with bare branches, will moderate the effects of heat loss, sites below trees offer good locations for plants like mountain laurel.

You may assume that the southern side of a house is a preferred location for laurels. Not so. Plants on the southern side of a building are exposed to the full winter sun and reflected heat in the day and then cruelly and suddenly subjected to the cold-air temperatures of night.

Excessively high daytime temperatures and frozen ground can literally be death to broad-leaved evergreens, because water is lost from the leaves and cannot be replaced from the roots (Figure 7–3). But a southern exposure can be tempered to the plant's benefit if it is moved several feet away from the building or if overhead trees break up the sun's intensity. The angle of the sun changes greatly during the year, so do not be fooled: Trees that shade a bed in June may not do an effective job in December.

The northern side of the house is one of the best locations for mountain laurel. Here the plants are shaded in winter because of the low sun angle, daytime temperatures are moderated, and the ground is subjected to less freezing and thawing. In summer they receive early morning and late afternoon sun but are shaded from the intense midday sun.

Ground slope is not of prime importance as long as other conditions are met. A southern slope is warmer and dryer than one facing north; hence on the former a good mulch is essential.

Eastern bog laurel, mountain laurel, and sheep laurel are all

Figure 7–3 (A) The rolled and drooped leaves of a rhododendron on a cold day with the temperature below freezing. (B) Mountain laurel leaves do not roll but will droop as the temperature drops to teens. Note flower buds on both plants.

found fairly close to the coastline, but only the eastern bog laurel and sheep laurel can be considered salt-tolerant. Mountain laurel can not withstand salt and in the Northeast, where roads are kept clear in winter with applications of sodium chloride, plants close to the road have often died. Where mountain laurel survives along such roads it is either up a bank or out beyond the splash or drainage zone of the road bed.

SOIL

Laurels prefer a well-drained, acid soil and suffer in heavy, poorly drained, alkaline soils. Bog laurel and sheep laurel can tolerate wet soil but do better in well-drained locations. Fortunately, inhospitable soils can be modified. Peat moss, up to 50 percent by volume, can be mixed into clayey soils and the planting bed raised a few inches to improve drainage and aeration. Peat moss will improve most soils and aid in establishing new transplants.

In clayey soils, prepare an area much larger and deeper than that required for the root ball and work in peat moss, leaf mold or other partially decayed organic matter. A shallow, dish-like hole in such soils acts as a catch basin for rain water and the roots will rot.

Plant growth depends on soil moisture; soils vary greatly in their water-holding capacity and their ability to release water to plants. Coarse, sandy soils admit water rapidly but have limited storage capacity. Fine textured soils, on the other hand, have a much larger capacity, but when compacted water infiltration is slow and surface runoff increased. In addition, water is tightly held to fine clay particles, and therefore less moisture is released to plant roots in clayey soils than in sandy soils.

Established laurels are fairly tolerant of drought conditions but will obviously do best when soils are kept moist. Conditions vary, but during the growing season plants need approximately 1 inch of water per week; if not released by the soil or provided by rains, then irrigation is necessary. Since daily waterings may waterlog the soil, and sprinklings may be superficial, a good soaking every one to two weeks during dry periods is preferred.

pH is the term applied to the chemical measure of the hydrogen ion concentration of the soil solution. Neutrality is pH 7.0. Acid soils have a numerical value lower than seven; alkaline soils have a numerical value higher than seven. Few natural soils are more acid than pH 3.5 or more alkaline than pH 9.0. Where laurels are found, the pH generally ranges between 4.0 and 5.5.

If the soil pH is 5.6 or higher, an acidifying material such as aluminum sulfate, ferrous sulfate, or finely divided sulfur should be added to lower the pH. The following table gives approximate figures of the amount needed to increase the acidity (lower the pH) for silty loams. On coarse sandy soils, 50 percent less material should be applied.

To change pH			Pounds of material per 100 square feet		
Start		Desired	Aluminum sulfate	Ferrous sulfate	Sulfur
8.0	to	5.5	13.5	25.9	5.5
7.5	to	5.5	11.5	23.5	5.0
7.0	to	5.5	9.0	16.5	3.5
6.5	to	5.5	6.5	11.8	2.5
6.5	to	5.0	10.5	18.8	4.0

If aluminum sulfate is used excessively, aluminum toxicity may occur in some soils. David Leach, in his book, *Rhododendrons of the World*, strongly recommends ferrous sulfate, but the average garden center or nursery supplier does not stock this material. You must go to chemical supply houses. The price should be about the same as aluminum sulfate. Both sulfates are quick-acting, two to three weeks, compared with six to nine weeks for sulfur. Although slow acting, sulfur is less expensive and longer lasting.

Soils are formed over long time periods from various materials such as limestone and sandstone. Parent rocks determine the soil pH in the first place, and, even though additives can modify it, it always tends over a period of time to return to its original pH. Foundation soils often end up with too high a pH for ericaceous plants, because calcium leaches from the concrete walls or because plaster or other limestone material was left in the soil at the time of construction. Even the careless application of lime to an adjacent lawn can have a similar effect.

FERTILIZER

Normal plant growth depends on at least fourteen elements supplied by the soil. Of these, nitrogen (N), phosphorus (P), potassium (K), calcium (Ca), magnesium (Mg), and sulfur (S) are required in sufficient quantities to be called major or macronutrients. The remainder, including iron (Fe), boron (B), and zinc (Zn), are utilized by plants in small quantities and are called minor or micronutrients. Deficiencies or excesses in either major or minor nutrients can cause abnormal growth and may even be fatal to the plants.

Most soils contain less than optimal amounts of one or more of the elements, and one must determine these to know when fertilizer is needed. Obviously fertilizer is needed if the amount of new growth and color of foliage are poor. Composition and vigor of weeds are also good indicators, or the soil or leaves may be chemically analyzed.

Plants in good, nutritious soils have a lustrous green to blue green color, good growth, and good leaf retention. Those in poor soils grow slowly, have poor color, and lose their leaves. The excess of nutrients may cause leggy, "floppy" growth and eventually injure the roots, leaves, and shoots. The state of vigor and the composition of weeds are usually obvious but are more difficult to diagnose in terms of soil fertility.

Soil testing is the most reliable means to measure soil fertility. Soil testing services are available through most state universities and experiment stations, and some private firms test soil; or kits are available to do your own testing. Information on who does soil testing and how to take samples can be obtained from county agricultural extension agents or the nearest state university.

Laurels can exist under conditions of very low fertility and thrive with moderate fertilization. Applications should never exceed the amounts recommended for rhododendrons or hollies. Err in the direction of too little, because more laurels have been injured by excessive fertilization, especially nitrogen applications, than from nutrient starvation. Those who test your soil will suggest what kind and how much fertilizer to apply. If plant growth suggests the need for fertilizer and a soil test is not readily obtainable, then use the rates suggested on bags of commercially available fertilizers for acid-loving plants. Were you to use one of the common evergreen plant foods commercially available, and containing 8-percent nitrogen, 4-percent phosphorus and 4-percent potassium, (8-4-4) the rate of application is 2 pounds per 100 square feet, or 800 pounds per acre. Sixteen percent of this fertilizer is active ingredients (three macronutrients) and the remaining 84 percent is inert. Cottonseed meal has an analysis of 7-3-2 and can be applied at the same rate as the 8-4-4 fertilizer. Two or three light applications of fertilizer at intervals are preferable to a single heavy application, especially when the nitrogen is in a readily soluble form. Even the "slow-release" fertilizers must be applied conservatively around laurel.

TRANSPLANTING

Early fall and early spring are the best times for transplanting laurel, although with certain precautions they can be moved any time that the ground is not frozen. Fall transplanting has some advantages over spring transplanting if the move is made early. Take the following precautions to prevent frost heaving: Choose a site with well-drained porous soil and use wood chips or other mulch. Fall plantings put in at least a month before the ground freezes will have well established roots when spring shoot growth occurs. For, despite the dormant top, the roots may remain active as long as the temperatures are above freezing. Nurserymen and experienced gardeners have long taken advantage of this phenomenon to give their plants a head start.

All plants suffer some degree of shock from transplanting, since no specimen, whether field or container grown, can be transplanted without some disturbance to the roots. Container-grown plants suffer less root loss, but they must adjust to a great difference between the texture of the mix within the container and the soil they are placed in. Such differences between mix and soil inhibit water exchange and root growth. To facilitate the outward growth of the roots and the assimilation of water, make several shallow vertical cuts into the root ball of container-grown plants before placing them in the hole.

Next to fall transplanting, early spring is best. Winter transplanting is possible in regions where the ground does not freeze solidly. Take extra care whenever transplanting to obtain a good root ball, and never let the ball dry out. When there is a large amount of soft growth or the roots have been severely disturbed, prune the top growth to lessen water loss through the foliage.

MULCH

Native laurels usually grow where they have at least some natural mulch around them, so you should always provide a good mulch for the ones in your garden. Mulches limit the growth of weeds, conserve soil moisture, decrease leaching and erosion, moderate soil temperature, prevent compaction, and, as organic mulches decompose, they release nutrients to the soil.

Wood chips and pine bark are two excellent mulches, but many others are often available locally, such as sugar-cane bagasse or buckwheat hulls. Peat moss is usually not satisfactory, because the surface dries and mats, becoming almost waterproof, and worse, if fluffed up, it blows away. Hays and straws are good, but weed seeds in them can cause a serious nuisance. (I stopped using salt marsh hay after one particularly weedy bale cost me many hours of back-breaking work.) The leaves collected by municipalities are an inexpensive substitute for bark or wood chips. I have truckloads dumped at my home in the fall; by spring they are quite usable. One drawback is that they do not last as long as chips and blow away in windy locations. But if you grind them up, they have a more uniform appearance and do not blow away as readily. Nonorganic mulches such as stone and gravel may be desirable in formal settings. Fresh sawdust or fine, new wood chips work well, but initial bacterial action on them may tie up free nitrogen. So, if you use such organic mulches, add a light side dressing of nitrogen. As organic mulches decay (compost), they release the nitrogen that was earlier unavailable.

Soil pH may be raised, lowered, or unaffected by mulch. Sandy soils with low organic content have their pH most easily changed. Organic mulches rich in calcium, magnesium, and potassium (such as maple leaves) tend to increase pH, whereas mulches rich in tannins or other organic acids (such as oak leaves) decrease it. However, such changes are normally very gradual and unimportant. By contrast, the leaching of calcium from masonry walls has a more significant effect on changing pH.

Mulches control weeds and evaporation, and they permit more water to percolate through the soil. But, despite this potential for increased leaching, organic mulches increase available nitrate nitrogen, potassium, magnesium, and phosphorus. Fungi and bacteria increase under a mulch; apparently beneficial types prosper more than pathogenic ones. In addition, mulch protects and feeds earthworms (a valuable garden ally) against freezing and desiccation.

WEED CONTROL WITH HERBICIDES

A good mulch can solve the worst of your weed problems, and regular, but sparing, hand weeding will complete the job. I do not recommend chemical weed killers for most home gardeners. Yet, selected herbicides are necessary in large gardens, and commercial growers would find it difficult to continue without them. The expenditure of more money on herbicides than on either fungicides or insecticides indicates how important they have become.

A short overview will acquaint you with some of the herbicides that can be used around laurel. Since no single herbicide will control all weeds safely, your choice will depend on many factors, including size and type of plants, kinds of weeds, and time of year. Some products are designed for the home gardener; others should be used only by professionals. New materials enter the market constantly, and preferences and the laws governing use change. Because of this, before you purchase any herbicides, check with your extension service, state university, or other agricultural authority for the latest information on materials and proper usage in your locality.

Classification of Herbicides Based on Activity

PREEMERGENCE HERBICIDES   Because their action affects the weeds at such an early stage of growth, these chemicals are referred to as preemergence herbicides. They are selective in their effect on different kinds of plants. Crabgrass killers used on established lawns and applied in the spring are of this preemergence type. They are long lasting, having an effect for a few months to a year or more depending on the material and rate of application.

Simazine (Princep) is one of the most useful preemergence herbi-

cides and is sold as an 80-percent wettable powder (80W) or a
·4-percent granular preparation (4G). It kills many weeds as they
germinate and is also effective on many established weeds and
grasses when applied during the dormant season. Simazine is safe
when used around established plants if applied properly but may
lead to injury when applied around new transplants or small
seedlings. It has a residual action throughout the growing season
and a small persistent residue into the second year. The effect of
simazine can be improved by applying it along with other preemergence herbicides such as DCPA (Dacthal), diphenamid
(Dymid or Enide), and trifluralin (Treflan). These are more effective on grasses and some of the large-seeded, broad-leaved weeds
and are also packaged in wettable or granular forms. Like simazine,
DCPA and diphenamid are applied on the soil surface before weed
germination. Trifluarlin, on the other hand, is volatile and must be
mixed into the soil for best results. These materials have moderate
residual activity but when applied at the proper rates will not leave
soil residues harmful to the growth of laurel.

POSTEMERGENCE HERBICIDES   Dichlobenil (Casoron) is effective on
established perennial weeds in established plantings. Nurserymen
use it, but, unfortunately it injures the roots of recently planted
laurel. Applications are usually made on the soil surface during the
late fall, winter, or early spring when soil and air temperatures
are low.

METABOLIC INHIBITORS OR REGULATORS   Nonselective and systemic,
these act by upsetting the normal hormonal balance of the plant.
Examples are amitrole (Weedazol, Cytrol) and the phenoxy compounds 2,4-D and 2,4,5-T. They are effective against most perennial,
broad-leaved plants, both herbaceous and woody, and are the compounds commonly suggested for use on poison ivy. They are most
often applied in water sprays to the leaves so that the chemical is
absorbed and translocated to roots. Phenoxy herbicides can also be
applied in fuel oil or kerosene as a bark or stump treatment. Because
these nonselective herbicides are toxic to laurel itself, they are used
in killing brush and weeds prior to planting laurel or as a directed
spray around established plants. They do not have long residual
effects in the soil.

CONTACT HERBICIDES These nonselective, fast-acting herbicides break down rapidly and destroy plant membranes. Because of their action they are called "chemical hoes." They are most effective in preparing new planting beds that are in sod or annual weeds. One or two sprays eliminate the grass and weeds without spading or cultivation, and, because of their rapid breakdown, planting can be done within a day.

Paraquat is used commercially and is effective in combination with residual herbicides such as simazine and Dacthal. Applied as a directed spray, it kills established annual weeds and the tops of perennial grasses on contact, while the other two chemicals prevent regrowth of grass and kill germinating seed. We have used this combination successfully for many years now. Mix the material in 3 gallons of water, and apply it as a directed spray from a 3½-gallon backpack sprayer. Paraquat can cause serious injury to membranes of the lungs and eyes; hence, caution must be used in applying it. The homeowner needs a similar but safer chemical hoe than Paraquat in his fight against herbaceous weeds.

FUMIGANTS These are general sterilants used for treating soil. Fumigants such as metham (Vapam) and methyl bromide (Dowfume) have value in sterilizing soil for mixes or in treating beds prior to planting seedlings. They kill not only weed seeds but also perennial root stocks, fungi, and nematodes. The expense of fumigants generally precludes treating of large areas. For information on their use consult local agricultural authorities.

REMOVAL OF FADED FLOWERS
AND DEBUDDING OF MOUNTAIN LAUREL

Flower buds for the following year's bloom form in August and September on the current season's growth. Hence, cultural methods that increase the number of new shoots increase the potential for flower bud set. Flowers left on a shoot normally produce seed capsules and inhibit new growth on that shoot. Removal of the flower cluster immediately after flowering generally results in the formation of one or several new shoots, and on these new flower buds may form (Figure 7–4). New growth does not guarantee flowers the next year, but without new growth there will be no

Figure 7–4 The effect, by the end of summer, of "deadheading" in June. Flowers on left were allowed to form seed capsules. On right, flower cluster was broken out of the branch immediately after flowering. Four shoots developed, and two have flower buds for the next year.

flower bud set at all. The developing seed capsules not only limit new shoot growth, but evidence from work with other plants suggests that they produce a hormone which, when translocated to vegetative shoots, inhibits the formation of flower buds. This perhaps explains why mountain laurels tend to have good floral displays every other year and why the removal of developing seed capsules enhances annual flowering. The presence of seed capsules does not seem to have as strong an inhibiting effect on flower bud formation with the other laurel species.

Some people find plants with seed capsules unsightly, whereas others see them as an attractive feature of the plant. The hybrids may or may not have special merit, then, depending on your point of view, for they all, except for a few crosses of western laurel and eastern bog laurel, are sterile and fail to develop large persistent seed capsules.

Occasionally a mountain laurel will have flower buds on all the shoots when transplanted, or the shock of transplanting will subsequently result in an overabundance of flower buds. When this happens, too much of the plant's energy goes into flower and seed production and not enough into producing new growth for maintaining the plant in good condition. At least some of the flower buds should be removed to stimulate vegetative growth. If this cannot be done in the spring, the faded flowers should be removed immediately after flowering. Removal at the base of the plant stimulates branching and fullness at the base. Removal of flower buds only on top of the plant stimulates height growth.

PRUNING MOUNTAIN LAUREL

One of the most common questions is, "My foundation planting has become leggy; how and when do I prune it?" The answer is, "In early spring, before growth starts." This is the best time, although some flower buds will inevitably be removed. A second choice would be immediately after flowering, still early enough in the growing season to obtain at least one flush of growth subsequent to the pruning.

Pruning is an art; each plant has to be handled a bit differently, but there are some general rules. First, try to imagine what you want the plant to look like, and then prune with this design in mind. Do not prune back to naked, unbranched stems. Pruning cuts should be made at forks and where small laterals exist as sources of additional growth. There is little problem on plants with dense foliage all the way to the ground. Plants 4 to 6 feet tall without lower branches present a problem. There are two approaches, neither ideal, but both better than cutting the tops off and leaving 2- to 3-foot naked stems. One is to remove the plants and replace them with smaller bushes of desired size; this is drastic but gives immediate results. The other approach is to cut the overgrown plants to within 2 to 3 inches of the ground. They will resprout and form a dense multi-stemmed bush, but it may take three to four years for them to reach flowering size again.

Judicious pruning every year is the best way to prevent plants from getting leggy or too large. Since laurel foliage is attractive at all times of the year in flower arrangements and especially at Christmas time in decorations, you have enough excuse to prune the plants. Thinning out or removal of odd branches can be done any

Figure 7–5 Mountain laurel used as a hedge on perimeter of front lawn. Flowering dogwood trees add accent.

time of the year with no harmful effects on the plant. Mountain laurel is normally a graceful and informally shaped plant; older plants take on an exotic or oriental character. But it is also amenable to shearing and shaping and can be grown in dense mounds or in formal hedges (Figure 7–5). Such pruning should be done immediately after flowering to allow for new shoot growth and flower bud formation for the next year. However, in most situations the more natural, informal appearance that results from occasional, judicious pruning is far more attractive.

A NOTE ON THE HARVESTING OF
MOUNTAIN LAUREL FOLIAGE

Fifty years ago, Buttrick estimated that 10,000 tons (20 million pounds) of laurel foliage were used annually in the United States for decorations during the holiday season. Since the estimated average yield per acre was as low as one-fourth ton, nearly 40,000 acres were cut over annually for laurel foliage. A new crop could be harvested from the same land every five years. Thus, a total of 120,000 acres would grow indefinitely all the laurel required by the trade. Obviously this is but a small fraction of the total area where laurel is presently growing.

Buttrick wrote:

The growing of laurel for the sale of its foliage would be quite different from its cultivation for ornamental use in gardens. Its production for market could best take place in woodland, [where] advantage would be taken of its sprouting power. No attempt would be made to grow it from seed or to produce large and handsome clumps.

The cutting of laurel so that it will sprout satisfactorily and produce further crops is quite simple. Ordinarily collectors cut or break it off at about eighteen inches back from the tips of the branches. Inferior branches are apt to be left growing. A good second growth seldom follows such a cutting. To secure a good second crop the cut should be made close to the root and those parts of the plant not useful for decorating purposes should be discarded.

No statistics are available, but laurel greens are still used extensively in florists' arrangements throughout the year. The trade in laurel foliage has diminished considerably since Buttrick's time, in large part because of high labor costs for harvesting and certainly because of restrictive and misunderstood state laws. Most states prohibit pruning and digging of laurel on state lands and public rights of way. Laurel is specifically mentioned in the laws of Pennsylvania, Connecticut, New Jersey, and North Carolina and is protected by more general statutes in other states.

Misunderstanding of these laws is widespread. Some private landowners, for example, wonder whether or not they have the right to move, or even prune, laurel on their own property. Of course they can! In fact, the judicious harvesting of laurel foliage for floral decoration could well supplement a landowner's income. Discretionary pruning does no harm and often helps the plants. Pruning is a common method of keeping cultivated plants in bounds.

There are other interesting uses of laurel. A century ago in England, mountain laurel was forced in the greenhouse as a pot plant. There is no reason why today the several species, their hybrids, and the newer selections should not be experimented with for pot culture and possibly forced for cut flowers. Exhibitors in the Boston and Philadelphia spring flower shows (held in March and April) show mountain laurel in bloom. Such plants are usually brought into a cool enclosure around Christmas and are gradually exposed to an increasingly warm temperature over a period of many weeks. Care is needed, however, for if they are forced with a too high temperature, they lose their flower color.

Rules of the Federated Garden Clubs add to the mystique and taboo of laurel use, for they have stipulated that mountain laurel flowers and foliage cannot be used by their members in arrangements which are entered for competitive judging. This is unfortunate, since we now have many cultivated varieties of mountain laurel which are unknown in the wild. I do not question the intent of the rule but believe it should be changed to allow the use of laurel foliage and flowers, at least from cultivated plants, as well as native plants from one's own property. What better, more pleasing way to appreciate and enjoy this handsome plant?

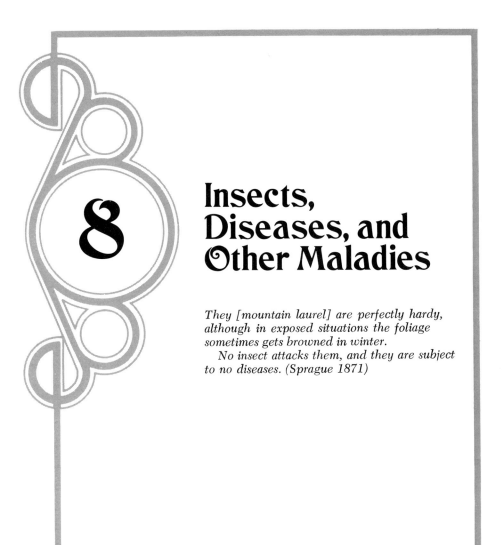

8

Insects, Diseases, and Other Maladies

They [mountain laurel] are perfectly hardy, although in exposed situations the foliage sometimes gets browned in winter.

No insect attacks them, and they are subject to no diseases. (Sprague 1871)

Every plant is subject to the ever-present threat of harm from insects and diseases; although the laurels, when grown under the proper conditions, are relatively free of such threats, problems do occur. So here we describe the common threats to laurels and methods to control them. I shall concentrate on mountain laurel pests but will not neglect those with a preference for the other species.

Since things change rapidly, the materials listed here may or may not be available at the time you read this book, so always check with local authorities. Consult local agricultural experts for current registered uses of pesticides, and be sure to read and follow instructions on pesticide labels.

INSECTS AND MITES

Lacebug, *Stephanitis rhododendri* and *S. pyrioides*

Adults and nymphs of the lacebug feed by inserting their mouth parts and sucking sap from the undersides of the leaves (Figure 8–1). Their feeding shows on the upper leaf surface as a mottle

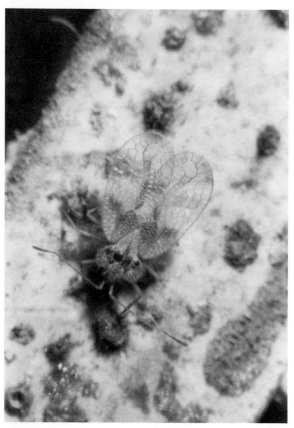

Figure 8–1   Lacebug on the underside of a sheep laurel leaf. Excrement spots on leaf surface are characteristic of lacebug infestation.

of numerous whitish specks, not unlike the damage caused by leaf-hoppers and mites on other plants. On the undersurface the leaf becomes brown-spotted with excrement. The lacebugs pass the winter in the form of eggs attached to the underside of the leaf, usually near the midrib. They hatch in May, and the nymphs mature in June. Eggs for the second brood are laid in June and July and hatch in August. This generation of nymphs matures late in the season, and the adults lay eggs on the leaves; these eggs overwinter there and hatch the following spring. Mountain laurel and sheep laurel plants grown in full sun are the most commonly attacked. Fortunately the lacebugs are seldom the problem on laurel that they are on the related Japanese andromeda, *Pieris japonica.*

Control these pests by spraying the undersides of the leaves with Sevin, which kills both nymphs and adults. The first spraying should be in late May before mountain laurel flowers and the second in July or whenever lacebugs are noticed.

Blackvine and Strawberry Weevils, *Brachyrhinus sulcatus* and *B. ovatus*

Adult weevils feed at night, cutting notches along the margin of the leaves. Larvae or grubs devour small roots and gnaw the bark from larger roots, often girdling them. Adults can be killed with foliar sprays of chlordane applied between June 15 and July 20 (dates will vary in different areas where laurel grows, but, in general, the best time is a few weeks immediately after flowering). Grubs can be killed by a ground application of the same material. Chlordane should be mixed into the soil by cultivation or by watering in order to expose the chemical to the roots, where the insects are active.

Mulberry Whitefly, *Tetraleurodes mori*

This insect attacks mountain laurel as well as numerous other plants, including mulberry. The oval nymphs or larvae appear on the undersides of the leaves and are dark brown or black, fringed with a whitish border composed of a waxy secretion. Damage of these insects does not usually warrant control measures, but they can be destroyed with a synthetic pyrethrin (SBP-1382, Resmethrin).

Cankerworms, Gypsy Moths, Other Leaf Eaters

Inchworm, cankerworms, caterpillars, specifically gypsy moths (*Porthetria dispar*), and elm spanworms (*Ennomos subsignarius*) are not supposed to "enjoy" laurel foliage. However, dietary preference goes out the window when populations of these insects reach epidemic levels. Laurels under trees which have been defoliated by these larvae are soon attacked. Control with sprays of Sevin, methoxychlor, or the bacterium *Bacillus thuringiensis* (Dipel) at ten-day intervals when the larvae are present.

Rhododendon Borer, *Ramosia rhododendri*

This borer prefers rhododendrons but also attacks mountain laurel. The larvae bore under the bark on main stems, leaving scars and sometimes girdling or weakening branches. The moths appear in May and June and the females lay their eggs on the twigs. The moth has clear wings spreading about ½ inch. Injured stems should be removed and burned. To prevent damage, the larger stems can be sprayed or painted with an insecticide (check on registration of lindane and methoxychlor) at twenty-day intervals starting in mid-May. Apply two or three treatments.

Leaf Rollers or Leaftiers, *Archips* species

The larvae roll the young leaves around themselves, hold the leaf in place with webbing, and then proceed to feed on it. They also enter the flower buds and eat the pollen from the anthers, disfiguring the flowers and making them shorter-lived. This is a particularly vexing pest when one is attempting to make cross-pollinations and nearly every bud is injured and has had the pollen eaten by leaftiers. The same materials listed for other leaf eaters will control them. Apply spray several days before the flowers open so that flower-visiting bumblebees will not be affected.

Seed Eaters and Other Insects

In addition to the leaf roller that thrives on the pollen of laurel flowers, another larva or later generation of the same leaf roller is a notable predator of the seeds in developing seed capsules, a particularly cursed beast for the plant breeder. Repeated dustings of the developing seed capsules with an insecticide such as malathion at ten-day intervals control the damage.

Aphids, *Neoamphorophora kalmiae* and Others

Aphids are sucking insects and generally are only a problem on succulent new foliage. If large numbers are present, they stunt and deform new growth. They have been a problem on young green-house-grown plants of bog laurel and on young mountain laurel plants in shaded beds. They can be controlled with malathion applied as a spray or with some of the systemics applied as drenches.

European Red Mite, *Metatetranychus ulmi*

Mites are not usually a problem on mountain laurel but they do occur, in fact regularly on our western laurel and eastern bog laurel. The most serious problems have been on cuttings of mountain laurel placed in polyethylene-covered propagation cases. Such extremely humid conditions are not normally associated with mite infestations, but their buildup in propagation beds might be explained by the lack of natural predators.

Mature mites are extremely small and are best seen using a magnifier (Figure 8–2). They feed by sucking plant juices. The adult female European red mite is dark red with white spots. Mites pass the winter in the egg stage on bark. Several generations develop each summer with peak infestations occurring in mid- to late summer. Mites have tremendous reproductive abilities and can rapidly reach epidemic proportions. (In four weeks at 80°F, a female mite is capable of giving rise to well over 13 million mites.) Infested foliage takes on a mottled, bronze cast, and affected leaves may drop prematurely. Several miticides, including Kelthane and Tedion, can be applied as a spray. Systemics are also effective applied as a soil drench.

Miscellaneous

Other insects and mites may cause problems from time to time. Local agricultural extension agents will help in identifying them and in suggesting controls.

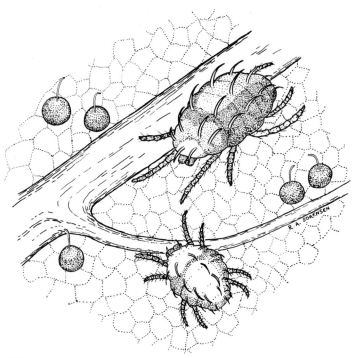

Figure 8–2 Mites and eggs on the underside of a laurel leaf. The adults are only about the size of the period at the end of this sentence and often go unnoticed until leaves become discolored.

DISEASES
Leaf Spot

The fungus *Mycosphaerella colorata*, also referred to by its conidial stage, *Phyllosticta kalmicola*, causes irregular, light gray spots with a red to purplish brown border. At first the spots are red and small but increase up to ½ inch in diameter. Tiny black pustules (fruiting bodies) are scattered over the infected areas. The leaves are unsightly and, when severely infected, fall prematurely. The disease is most common on mountain laurel when the bushes are crowded or shaded; under such conditions humidity can be high, and moisture on the foliage does not evaporate readily after rains or heavy dews.

Whenever possible, collect all fallen and infected leaves and burn or remove them from the area. Increase the amount of light and air circulation around crowded, shaded plants by removing low over-hanging tree branches and competing vegetation. Where leaf spot was serious the previous year, spray new growth when half devel-oped with a fungicide and repeat the spray when the leaves are fully developed. Use benomyl (Benlate), captan, ferbam, thiram, or zineb.

Leaf Blight

This fungal disease is caused by *Diaporthe kalmiae*, also known in the conidial stage as *Phomopsis kalmiae*. The symptoms are circular brown zonate areas that become irregular in shape as they increase in size (Figure 8-3). They may eventually run together, covering the entire leaf blade. The blight also attacks stems and causes branches to die. The disease appears to be most common, like leaf spot, when new foliage remains moist for long periods. Control this the same way you would leaf spot (as explained above).

Figure 8-3 Leaf blight on mountain laurel as seen on upper and lower leaf surface. Leaf blight and leaf spot are fungal diseases.

Numerous other fungi cause spotting and blighting of laurel foliage. These include: *Cercospora kalmiae, C. sprasa, Septoria angustifolia, S. kalmicola, Venturia kalmiae, Physalospora kalmiae,* and *Pestalotia* sp. The latter has been found on petioles and leaves of sandhill laurel cuttings kept in a humidity case. Control of these leaf-attacking fungi is the same as that given above for leaf spot.

Petal Blight

Primarily a disease of azaleas, this can attack mountain laurel flowers during warm and humid flowering seasons. The fungus, *Ovulinia azalea,* attacks the flower corolla, which becomes limp when covered by the frost-like bloom of spores of the fungus. Control measures are not necessary unless the season is abnormally wet; zineb (Dithane Z-78), sprayed several times before and during flowering, will prevent petal blight.

Wilt or Root Rot

This is primarily a seedling or nursery disease, caused by *Phytophthora cinnamomi,* which attacks the roots of young plants. It is soil-borne. The most noticeable symptom is wilted foliage, which is easiest to detect in the early morning when healthy plants are turgid. Foliage becomes discolored and acquires an olive green cast. At first only one or two branches show symptoms. Tissue of the stem near the ground level will be dead and brown. If you scrape the bark along the stem, you will see a characteristic reddish band traveling up the vascular tissue. The band may be either thread-like or up to ½ inch across. *Phytophthora* wilt is almost always fatal to infected plants. It can occur among seedlings in the cutting bench and also in older plants grown in containers or in the field.

The disease is most active in warm weather and is common in cases where aeration of the roots is poor and soil pH is high. Although the plants may grow best at pH 5.5, the fungus can be combated by increasing acidity to pH 4.5. Roots dead from waterlogging or injured during transplanting or similar root damage open the way for infection. Container-grown plants allowed to sit in puddles of water suffer not only from insufficient drainage but are susceptible to a motile spore stage of the fungus that can travel in the water from diseased to healthy plants.

Infected plants should be removed and destroyed. Soil and benches in greenhouses should routinely be fumigated or sterilized before any planting. Since freezing of the soil apparently destroys the disease, infected fields can be left fallow over winter. But diseased plants should be destroyed because the fungus winters oven in infected plant tissue. Several fungicides have been recommended for control of the disease, but none has yet proved to be consistently effective. *Phytophthora* is widespread and attacks many different kinds of plants, including *Rhododendron*, yew (*Taxus*), and chestnut (*Castanea*). Selection of resistant varieties may be one of the best long-term solutions. We have much to learn about the susceptibility of laurel selections to *Phytophthora* and the means to develop resistant cultivars.

Damping-Off

The fungus *Rhizoctonia solani* (*Pellicularia filamentosa*) causes stem rot at the ground line. It can be very serious on young seedlings, especially when they are planted in soil mixes. The disease can be avoided to a large extent through the use of nonsoil mixes containing milled sphagnum and peat moss. These contain natural antibiotics that prevent, or limit, the growth of this fungus. Larger plants are also susceptible, notably where soil aeration is poor and when overwatering has occurred. As with wilt and some other soil pathogens, *Rhizoctonia* is associated with soils or mixes having a relatively high pH. For laurel the pH should normally not be over 5.5, and lower if damping-off or other diseases are a problem. The symptoms of *Rhizoctonia* are similar to those for *Phytophthora*. Roots are destroyed, but the reddish vascular streaks beneath the bark are not present. The disease can be controlled by drenching the soil with a fungicide such as benomyl.

Phythium, another damping-off fungus, attacks young seedlings. It is often noticed on seedlings that are grown in closed, humid chambers where they have been overwatered. Aeration and a less moist medium will help check its spread. Control with fungicides may be necessary, but apply them sparingly on the young seedlings.

Other fungi may attack laurel roots and cause symptoms similar to those of *Phytophthora* and *Rhizoctonia*. One example is shoestring root rot, *Armillaria mellea*. The causes for these diseases are often similar, but the most common cause of all is injured roots resulting from poor growing conditions such as overfertilization, winter injury, overwatering, and lack of aeration, any of which provide an opportunity for the diseases to take hold.

MISCELLANEOUS AFFLICTIONS
Winter Injury

This nonparasitic disease is characterized by browning of the leaves at their tips and around the edges. When severe, entire leaves and even branches may be killed. At first the foliage changes from the normal dark green to a light, dull green and subsequently to brown (Figure 8–4). Severe damage occurs when the roots are frozen solid and strong freezing winds dessicate the leaves. Injury is not confined

Figure 8–4 Winter injury on mountain laurel foliage with characteristic browning and dieback of leaf tips.

to the coldest periods in midwinter but often occurs in March, after warm periods, while the ground is still frozen. A good mulch applied over the roots in November to insulate the soil is one of the best preventive measures. Windswept locations should be avoided as planting sites. Such unfavorable locations are observed as bare patches after a blustery snow storm. Plants exposed to the buffeting of winter winds should be protected with snow fencing, pine boughs, burlap, or other means. Remove killed and injured portions of winter-damaged plants. If in doubt as to how much to prune off, wait until the new growth begins in the spring, and then prune back to the new shoots.

Container-grown plants in unheated, plastic overwintering structures may, like rhododendrons, suffer from water soaking of the leaves when well watered and kept warm and humid. Plants in this condition are then susceptible to damage by freezing. Good aeration around the plants during warm spells in the fall and conservative watering are two of the best preventives.

Sunscald

Sunscald may occur on either newly transplanted or established plants that were adapted to shade and then, later, are exposed to full sun and an inadequate water supply. The symptoms are bleaching of the chlorophyll on the upper surface of exposed leaves and eventual browning. Affected leaves and branches should be pruned. Acclimatization, through gradual exposure of shaded plants to full sun, is the practical preventive measure.

Frost Damage

Unusual cold in spring or fall may damage plants. In fall, an early hard frost will injure plants that have continued to grow and failed to "harden off." Normally the shorter days of fall and cool weather are signals to the plant to stop growth and to prepare for winter. However, a moist, rich soil and mild fall weather, especially after a hot dry summer, may delay normal dormancy and stimulate plant growth. Mulched, field-grown plants in low areas are particularly susceptible, because the mulch slows up heat and water loss from the ground and helps maintain root growth and, as previously noted, cold air on still nights flows down a slope to the low areas. Thus the normally beneficial effects of a mulch are detrimental on a clear, still, frosty night. The air above the mulch supercools, because heat from the ground is trapped. The effect in spring is similar. This was dramatically illustrated a few years ago when we had a field of tomatoes planted adjacent to some established mountain laurel that were mulched with wood chips. On a clear evening late in May, our weather station recorded a low of 35°F, and, indeed, the tomatoes over the bare soil came through the night with no damage. New growth on much of the mountain laurel, however, was killed. The heat rapidly radiated off the wood chips; the air actually cooled to the freezing point, causing the laurel shoots to freeze, but the air around the tomatoes over the bare, moist soil was kept warmer by a constant supply of heat escaping upward from the soil.

The moral of this story is that heavy organic mulches may lead to frost injury in low pockets with poor air drainage. Such frost damage seldom occurs under a canopy of evergreen, or even deciduous, trees, because the canopy reflects radiated heat back to the ground.

An early hard freeze may not only destroy succulent branch tips but also actually split the bark on stems and kill the plant to the ground. Such damage may not be noticeable until the following spring when the top of the plants dries up. Measures that acclimate plants in the fall include removal of heavy mulch until after a hard freeze and no heavy fertilization or watering in late summer and early fall.

Chlorosis

One of the most common troubles encountered with laurels is chlorosis or yellowing of the leaves. The symptoms are first found on the youngest leaves; the leaf veins typically remain green (Figure 8–5). On severely affected plants the leaves may turn white before drying up. The problem is often caused by soil with a pH of 6.0 or higher, which converts iron into a form that is unavailable to the plant. Lowering the pH with aluminum sulfate is relatively simple (see page 66).

Chlorosis symptoms also result from causes other than high pH,

Figure 8–5 Chlorosis shows yellowing between veins, which remain green. An effect often seen due to root injury or growing plants in neutral or alkaline soil.

including fertilizer root burn from too much nitrogen and winter injury of roots. Immediate reversal of symptoms can often be achieved by applying iron in the chelated form (such as Sequestrene) either as a drench or foliage spray. But the actual cause of the chlorosis should be determined by examining the growing site and the plant, testing the soil, and taking additional corrective measures when necessary.

Despite the preceding list of a multitude of pests, be assured that they are not often serious on laurel. However, an awareness of potential problems and their early control is important in limiting serious depredations.

Toxicity of Laurel Foliage*

From Pehr Kalm's entries in his journal, which he started publishing in 1753, we know of many early uses of the mountain laurel, most of which the settlers learned from the Indians. When Kalm was in America, the laurel was already being grown in colonial gardens as an ornamental. The evergreen branches of this shrub were used as church decorations at Christmas and New Year's Day. Its usefulness was the primary reason for its importance, however. The strong wood was carved into weaver's shuttles, pulleys, and spoons and trowels. The early common name spoonwood indicates this usefulness for tools. The leaves also were valued for their supposed medicinal powers, especially when prepared as a wash for skin diseases. (Holmes 1956)

In 1743 Mark Catesby was one of the first to report the poisonous properties of mountain laurel, *Kalmia latifolia*. He found that, when deprived of better forage, cattle and sheep died from eating the leaves of this species. Later Peter Kalm wrote an extensive and interesting account of the appearance, habitat, and poisonous properties of both mountain laurel and sheep laurel, *K. angustifolia*. In

* Dr. John E. Ebinger, Eastern Illinois University, Charleston, Illinois.

this travelog, published in 1770, he mentioned that young sheep were killed by eating only small portions of the leaves of mountain laurel, while older sheep became very sick and recovered with great difficulty. He also observed that after calves ate the foliage of mountain laurel they would swell, foam at the mouth, and have difficulty standing. They could usually be cured by giving them gunpowder and other medicines. He reported that larger animals were also affected, but they usually recovered.

It is now known that many members of the Ericaceae contain a toxic substance. This chemical, andromedotoxin, has been isolated from some members of the family and has produced similar symptoms in most domestic animals. Most of the cases of andromedotoxin poisoning have occurred in the upland pastures of eastern North America and in the mountain ranges and coastal regions of the West, the areas where species of *Kalmia* are found. Since species of this genus are extremely common, and since some grow in habitats readily accessible to livestock, some cases of poisoning have been attributed to them. Also, their evergreen habit makes them readily available during the winter and early spring when other food is scarce.

Cases of andromedotoxin poisoning occur most frequently among sheep; cattle poisoning is second. In the eastern part of the United States the poisoning is usually caused by mountain laurel or sheep laurel. The eastern bog laurel, *K. polifolia*, is also poisonous but owing to its bog habitat is seldom encountered by livestock. Some experimental work has been done to determine the dosage, symptoms, and treatment for poisoning by these species. One of the first studies was made by Thomas Wood in 1883. He fed boiled extract of *K. angustifolia* leaves to a sheep. He concluded that extremely small quantities would not harm animals but that large quantities could cause sickness and death.

Recent studies confirm the poisonous properties of both mountain laurel and sheep laurel. In all experiments both species were found to be poisonous, producing almost identical symptoms. The major variable is the time from ingesting of the dosage to the appearance of the first symptoms. Symptoms usually appear in six hours, depending on the amount of foliage consumed. In order of appearance, the symptoms are lack of appetite, repeated swallowing, copious salivation, dullness, depression, and nausea. As the poisoning progresses, the animal becomes weak, is unable to coordinate voluntary muscular movements, and falls to the ground. Vomiting and bloat are also common. In fatal cases death is preceded by coma and occurs from a few hours to a week after the first symptoms appear.

Observations suggest that sheep laurel is about twice as toxic as mountain laurel. The minimum toxic dose for mountain laurel fed to sheep is 0.35 percent of the animal's weight, while for sheep laurel the minimum toxic dose is only 0.15 percent. Similar results were found with other animals tested. The minimum toxic dose of mountain laurel fed to cattle and goats is 0.4 percent of the animal's weight, while for sheep laurel the minimum toxic dose is 0.25 percent for goats and 0.2 percent for cattle.

At present no antidote is known for andromedotoxin poisoning. The ingesting of lard or oil hinders absorption of the poison while also acting as a purgative. This practice, used since colonial times, still gives the best results. The recommended dosage is 4 fluid ounces of linseed oil administered every two to three hours. In a recent experiment six sheep were given lethal doses of mountain laurel foliage, and all recovered after being treated with linseed oil.

Like its eastern relatives, the western alpine laurel, *K. microphylla*, is also poisonous. Because of its alpine habitat, this species from the northwestern part of North America is rarely encountered by livestock. Moreover, livestock will rarely eat it, but instances of sickness and death among lambs have been reported when they were admitted to the high range too early in the spring. Experiments with western alpine laurel revealed that both cattle and sheep could be poisoned; in fact, as little as 1 ounce of fresh leaves made sheep sick. Studies by A. B. Glawson show that sheep are affected by eating as little as 0.3 percent of their weight of alpine laurel foliage, but they may consume as much as 2 percent without being fatally poisoned. In all studies the symptoms were similar to those reported for livestock poisoning with other *Kalmia* species.

While there is now no doubt that most species of *Kalmia* are extremely poisonous, the number of domestic animals killed by these plants is fortunately not very great, in spite of the fact that the species are extremely common and grow in areas where livestock graze. As pointed out earlier, losses are small because the laurels are not very palatable and are therefore eaten only when other vegetation is scarce. This occurs when pastures have become overgrazed and little vegetation is left, or in the spring of the year after animals are turned into pastures in which the grasses have not had time to grow.

Most of the reports in the literature of *Kalmia* poisoning of live-stock occur under the circumstances described above. A recent case involved a number of newly bred ewes that died from sheep laurel poisoning in central Minnesota. The sheep in question had been im-ported from the West and were turned out in a 40-acre pasture with dense stands of sheep laurel. The day before losses were noted, the sheep had been fed no hay and only a limited supplemental feed. The next day the sheep were not fed at all, and they began to forage on the laurel since the ground was covered with snow and the evergreen sheep laurel was the only green foliage available (Figure 9–1). By the next morning all of the typical symptoms of andromedotoxin poisoning were observed among all the sheep, with the more severely ill animals going into coma and then death. Since

Figure 9–1   Sheep laurel, *Kalmia angustifolia*, in a snow-covered pasture. If other food is not available, stock may browse on it and become poisoned.

a marked reduction in intensity of heart sounds and heart rates was observed in these animals, the immediate cause of death was apparently circulatory collapse. Twenty-two of the fifty sheep in the flock died in three days. The animals that recovered did so within a week.

Other cases of laurel poisoning have resulted from the animals accidentally being fed the foliage or eating decorations made of mountain laurel leaves. For example, some cows were poisoned when they ate laurel wreaths that had been thrown into their pasture from a nearby cemetery. During Christmas week in 1894 six trained goats on exhibit at the Philadelphia Dime Museum died after browsing on laurel leaves that were being used as stage decorations. Angora goats were poisoned at the National Zoological Park in Washington, D.C., when they were fed mountain laurel leaves by a visitor. Later at the same park, a monkey died after eating a few flowers and leaves of mountain laurel offered to it by a visitor.

Reports from colonial times state that mountain laurel is poisonous to most domestic livestock but that many wild animals, particularly deer, can eat the leaves with impunity. Recent studies confirm that mountain laurel and rosebay, *Rhododendron maximum*, are sometimes eaten by deer, especially in times of food shortages. In experiments confined deer did not like either mountain laurel or rosebay and if given an alternative would eat very little of these plants. Furthermore, when restricted to a diet of these two species for forty-five days the deer did not eat enough of either plant to maintain their weight. They all became thin and weak, suffered from the cold, and developed a mild case of rickets. None of the deer, however, showed the typical symptoms of andromedotoxin poisoning. In related experiments deer exhibited the typical symptoms of andromedotoxin poisoning and died when force-fed 1.75 percent of their live weight of laurel leaves. Clearly, the toxic principle of both mountain laurel and rosebay is poisonous to deer, but they normally will not eat enough of either plant to exceed their tolerance for them.

Most species of *Kalmia* are probably poisonous to humans, but no deaths have been attributed directly to this genus. The first detailed study of human poisoning from mountain laurel was conducted by George C. Thomas in 1802. He found that, after eating very small quantities (0.4 to 1.0 grams) of dried leaves, some unpleasant symptoms resulted: rapid pulse, headache, throbbing of the temples, nausea, vomiting, and dilation of the pupils. Other cases have been reported in which a strong decoction (boiled extract) of leaves caused vertigo, dimness of sight, reduction in heartbeat, and cold extremities. In each instance the decoction was being used in an experiment to determine its effect on humans, or it was being used as a medicine. It is unlikely that anyone would eat the leaves under normal conditions, because they are tough and bitter. There are reports, however, that the Delaware Indians used a decoction of the leaves of mountain laurel to commit suicide.

Occasionally humans and other animals have become sick from eating birds whose crops contained the leaves and buds of mountain laurel. As a result, during the last century the common belief was that the flesh of birds feeding on mountain laurel was poisonous. In all cases, however, the reported symptoms were identical to those associated with food poisoning, and the probable cause of the discomfort was decomposition of the bird itself before it was cooked. There is no evidence that the flesh itself of any animal is made inedible by its eating any part of *Kalmia* species.

From colonial times until well into the last century, extracts from species of *Kalmia* have been used as medicine. The leaves of mountain laurel were occasionally found in drug stores and were principally used as a remedy for diarrhea. A decoction was made by softening 2 ounces of dried leaves in a pint of alcohol, letting it stand for a week, and then straining. The dosage customarily administered to an adult was 30 drops 4 times a day; stronger dosages caused vertigo. This preparation has also been used as a wash to relieve itching and skin infections and was recommended for use as a sedative, as well as a cure for syphilis and fever. Besides, the powder found in the leaves was popular as snuff.

Other species of *Kalmia* have also been used as medicine. The sheep laurel was used by the Cree Indians of the Hudson Bay region as a bitter tea both for the treatment of bowel complaints and as a tonic. The sandhill laurel has been used in the southeastern part of the United States as a cure for itching and mange in dogs. Treatment consisted of a strong decoction that was applied warm to the affected area. One application was enough to effect a cure. There are no reports that the other species of the genus have been used as medicine, though most of them contain the drug andromedotoxin.

Andromedotoxin is not being used as a drug today, although experiments indicate that it has potent hypotensive action. These studies revealed that intravenous injections of small quantities of the drug into normal dogs caused blood-pressure reductions of 20 to 40 percent.

A great deal of evidence indicates that when honeybees work certain members of the Ericaceae family, they produce a honey poisonous to humans. Xenophon reported that his soldiers suffered from honey poisoning while they were camped at Trebizond on the shores of the Black Sea in 400 B.C. He stated that those who had eaten small amounts of honey were merely intoxicated, while those who had eaten a great deal became madmen. It is believed that the honey was derived from *Rhododendron ponticum* which is now considered the chief source of poisonous honey in Asia.

In 1802, American botanist B. S. Barton observed that honey from sheep laurel is poisonous to humans. He reported that during the latter part of the seventeenth century a group of young men moved their beehives to the savannas of New Jersey during the flowering time of *Kalmia angustifolia*. On eating the honey produced, the men became intoxicated. Since this early report, a number of other cases of human poisoning have been reported in which species of *Kalmia* were suspected as the source of the honey. In all reported cases the honey acts as an extremely distressing narcotic, varying in its effect in proportion to the quantity eaten. The usual symptoms are nausea and vomiting and in extreme cases prostration and almost complete loss of the function of voluntary muscles. Since the honey produced is bitter and astringent, fatal amounts would rarely be eaten.

Some authors have expressed doubt that mountain laurel is responsible for poisonous honey. Since this species is common, contamination of honey might be expected much more often than is reported. On the other hand, honeybees are rarely found on mountain laurel. Possibly a certain set of environmental conditions are necessary before they will use mountain laurel flowers to produce honey. In none of the reported cases of poisoned honey is the source of the flowers for the honey known for certain.

In addition to possible effects on honey and animal poisoning from foliage, laurels may chemically limit growth of neighboring plants. Water-soluble extracts of northern sheep laurel inhibit the growth of coniferous trees and in nature may thereby maintain open areas for extended periods of time. The extracts hinder primary root development of black spruce by destroying cell tissues and may be the reason for the abnormally poor growth of trees associated with sheep laurel on upland sites in the boreal region of eastern Canada (Peterson 1965).

Chemical studies of the poison principle have been undertaken, mostly with genera of the Ericaceae other than *Kalmia*. The first detailed analysis was made by J. F. Eykman in 1882 using extracts from the Japanese andromeda, *Pieris japonica*. The physiologically active substance was named asebotoxin after the Japanese name of the plant. At about the same time, German chemist P. C. Plugge found the same substance in some species of *Andromeda* and *Rhododendron* and changed the name to andromedotoxin. By the beginning of this century Plugge extended the list of Ericaceae containing andromedotoxin to a number of species of *Andromeda*, *Pieris*, and *Rhododendron*, as well as the nongreen, herbaceous Indian pipe, *Monotropa unifolia*, and sheep laurel, *Kalmia angustifolia*. The list should be expanded to include western alpine laurel, *K. microphylla*, eastern bog laurel, *K. polifolia*, and mountain laurel, *K. latifolia*, and some members of the genera *Chamaedaphne*, *Leucothoe*, *Lyonia*, and *Pernettya*. Interestingly, some species of *Rhododendron*, *Lyonia*, and *Leucothoe* lack andromedotoxin, as does the sandhill laurel, *K. hirsuta*.

There is little agreement on the identity or the properties of the substance now commonly called andromedotoxin. In addition to the name asebotoxin (extracted from *Pieris japonica*), other names include rhodotoxin (from *Rhododendron hymenanthes*), grayanotocin I (from *Leucothoe grayana*), and acetylandromedol (from *Rhododendron maximum*). As for physical properties, the melting point, optical rotation, and crystalline structure of those reported all differ. Also, empirical formulas (chemical compositions) of $C_{19}H_{30-32}O_6$ to $C_{31}H_{51}O_{10}$ have been reported, although recent studies seem to indicate that $C_{22}H_{36}O_7$ is correct. It is not known whether several compounds of similar activity exist or whether the same compound is present in each of the species examined. Even a recent study, which showed that the physiologically active compounds extracted from many of the listed species have similar physical and chemical properties and may be identical, does not preclude the existence of a second compound with characteristics similar to andromedotoxin.

Renewed interest in andromedotoxin has led to the development of more exacting methods of isolating the compound. In one study 198 pounds of fresh leaves from rosebay, *Rhododendron maximum*, was used to produce ¼ ounce of andromedotoxin. Southern sheep laurel, *Kalmia angustifolia* var. *carolina*, is an even richer source of andromedotoxin. Large-scale isolation experiments show that 100 pounds of leaves of this species yield 1 ounce of andromedotoxin. Thus, southern sheep laurel yields 0.06 to 0.09 percent of the fresh weight or about ten times the amount obtained from rosebay. Small amounts of andromedotoxin can be extracted fairly simply with basic laboratory equipment.

Breeding
Better
Laurel

Gardeners have developed many interesting and beautiful varieties of rhododendrons by breeding and grafting. It would seem as though there would be an equal field for this with the mountain laurel, yet it does not appear to have attracted their attention in this respect. (Buttrick 1924)

The breeding and selection of improved types of laurel have just begun. Until my first paper was published in 1968 no literature on laurel breeding existed. By contrast, the literature on breeding azaleas and rhododendrons was extensive. Fewer than 100 *Kalmia* cultivars have been named, but hybridizers and growers of azaleas had named over 4800 cultivars in the 125 years prior to 1959, and that is to say nothing of all the hybridizing and selection done within the rhododendron section of the same genus. While there are fewer *Kalmia* than *Rhododendron* species, their variation is great, and therefore their potential for improvement by breeding is considerable.

10

Principles of Plant Breeding

In the beginning of June, when the days are long and warm and the daisies and clover in the tall grass are waving in the breeze, when the tulip-trees are in bloom and the roses and peonies fill the gardens with their perfume and color, then the flowers of the laurel may be found, rivalling in their delicacy of color and perfect symmetry of form any of the more showy blossoms of cultivation. It seems as if the climax of all that is dainty and lovely had been reached in this beautiful American wild flower. (Britton 1913)

Plants reproduce by either asexual or sexual means. Selected cultivars are usually reproduced by such asexual propagation methods as cutting, grafting, or layering. New cultivars, on the other hand, are usually selected from large populations grown from seed, that is, produced through sexual reproduction. Each seed produces a completely unique individual, differing to a greater or lesser degree from all others. The frequency and kind of variations in a population of seedlings depends on the parents. The more similar the parents, the more uniform the progeny. The plant breeder controls the traits expressed in the offspring not only by selecting the seed parent but also by selecting the pollen parent.

POLLINATION AND FERTILIZATION

Each seed results from the union of a male gamete (contained in a pollen grain) with a female gamete, the egg (contained in the ovule of the pistil) (Figure 10–1). Pollination, as we have learned, is normally carried out by bumblebees which bring the two gametes together; their union in the ovary is called fertilization. The male and female gametes contribute equally to the genetic content of the resulting seed. Thus, in a cross between two plants it does not matter which one is used as the female parent; the reciprocal crosses are

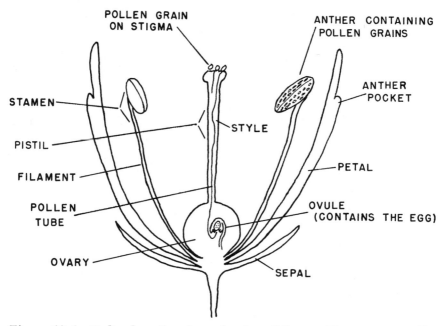

Figure 10–1   Stylized section through a laurel flower. The ovary actually contains many ovules; after fertilization these develop into seeds. Typical of all ericaceous plants, but not other flowering plants, the pollen grains are four-celled. Each is capable of producing four pollen tubes and fertilizing four eggs.

identical. Only rare exceptions occur. In laurel only albino and yellow sectoring in the foliage of mountain laurel are suspected of being dependent on maternal inheritance. However, reciprocal crosses are sometimes not equally successful, because pollen tube inhibition exists in the pistils of one plant. Some examples are cited in the next chapter.

SELF AND CROSS FERTILIZATION, INBREEDING AND OUTBREEDING

If the male gamete and the egg both come from the same plant or clone, the union is called self-fertilization or "inbreeding"; if from different clones, it is called cross-fertilization, or "outbreeding."

The laurels, like many woody plants, are predominantly outbreeders (outcrossers) in nature. The mechanism limiting self-fertilization in laurel has not been identified. It may result from inhibition of pollen tube growth in the style or, as my studies indicate, from inhibition at a later stage.

Inbreeding clearly causes a decrease in vigor. A 50-percent reduction in height growth of *Kalmia angustifolia, K. latifolia*, and *K. polifolia* after one generation was observed in inbred plants when compared with outbred ones. Inbreeding often results in greatly reduced seed set with *K. angustifolia* and *K. latifolia*.

The decreased vigor from inbreeding is caused by recessive traits which are normally masked by their dominant counterparts on outbreeding. True breeding, that is, lines that are completely uniform from generation to generation from selfing, would be difficult to develop because of inbreeding depression and the reduction in seed set. However, inbreeding, particularly of mountain laurel, may result in compact growing forms of ornamental value (Figure 10–2). These could be propagated vegetatively or by sibling crosses. Inbreeding uncovers recessive traits that may or may not have ornamental value. In natural outbreeding populations of laurel these recessive traits are normally hidden, but by chance recombination they are occasionally unmasked.

HYBRID VIGOR

A cross between two species or even between two plants within a species may produce offspring more vigorous than their parents.

Figure 10–2   Comparison of a four-year-old outbred and inbred mountain laurel, unpruned. The seed parent in both cases was the same. The plant on the left is typical of those from cross pollinations with another plant; the one on the right is characteristic of those obtained from self-pollination. (Jaynes 1968b)

This is hybrid vigor. Crosses between eastern bog laurel and western laurel (*K. polifolia* × *K. microphylla*) sometimes show hybrid vigor, usually expressed not as increased height growth but as a general thriftiness (well being).

CULTIVAR OR VARIETY SELECTION

Cultivars (varieties) of woody plants usually have been selected from wild populations or from seedlings grown in the garden. Such selected materials are commonly used to start breeding programs to develop improved cultivars (Figure 10–3). The plants judged to be the best garden sorts are the ones named, propagated, and introduced. Sometimes unusual plants are designated as botanical forms which may or may not have horticultural value. Feather-petaled (form *polypetala*) and banded (form *fuscata*) mountain laurels and

Figure 10–3 View of the Lockwood Farm of the
Connecticut Agricultural Experiment Station where
the author did much of his field research. A laurel
planting with a hemlock windbreak is in the
foreground, and Sleeping Giant State Park in the
background.

white flowering (form *candida*) sheep laurel are examples of
botanical forms. Several banded selections, in addition to 'Goodrich',
will undoubtedly receive cultivar names in the near future.

   The gradual, controlled improvement of mountain laurel has resulted from selecting and using seeds from desirable plants. The
deeply pigmented laurels (red-buds and pinks) originated in this

way. C. O. Dexter of Sandwich, Massachusetts, started with one or more good pinks collected in the wild. He grew several generations of seedlings and for each generation took the seed from the plants with the deepest flower color. This method of selection in gardens and nurseries has been effective (notably at Weston Nurseries, Hopkinton, Massachusetts) but inefficient, because, while the seed parent was known, the pollen parent was unknown. With controlled crosses both seed and pollen parents are known, and it is possible to determine how particular traits are inherited. This knowledge is valuable in planning the development of new cultivars and in reproducing desirable seed. Specific examples of gene inheritance are presented in the following chapters. Guidelines for naming plants appear in Chapter 3.

SPECIES HYBRIDIZATION

It is hard to overemphasize the point that variation is the key to plant breeding and selection. The greater the variation among crossed plants, the more likely that improved cultivars will develop. When the characteristics desired occur only in related species, one can resort to species hybridization. For instance, with mountain laurel it would be wonderful if a hybrid could be developed with general mountain laurel traits plus the solid, deep-wine-colored flowers of sheep laurel and the easy rooting characteristic of eastern bog laurel. Unfortunately, interspecific hybrids in laurel are difficult to create and when successful are often sterile—a disappointment, but not a total surprise since genetic barriers, if not the rule, are normal between species. Crosses above the species level, i.e., between genera, are seldom successful. As one could predict, crosses of *Kalmia* with the genera *Rhododendron* and *Kalmiopsis* have all failed with one notable exception: *K. latifolia* × *R. williamsonianum* (Chapter 11).

FIRST- AND SECOND-GENERATION CROSSES

The seedlings of a cross between two different plants or clones are referred to as first-generation, or F_1, hybrids. When two of these hybrids are then crossed, the offspring are called second-generation, or F_2, hybrids. To get the desired expression and recombination of characters, you must usually select among offspring of the second or later generations. For example, red-budded mountain laurel and feather-petaled mountain laurel are known to be controlled by recessive traits; thus, in a cross of these two kinds of mountain laurel, the F_1 would be expected to have normally colored and shaped flowers. A cross of two of these F_1 hybrids would produce a small proportion of seedlings exhibiting the unique combinations of red-buds and petaled corolla. The actual proportion of such plants would depend on the number of genes controlling these two traits, and this is yet to be determined for the red-bud character.

The odds of recovering the desired recombinant in the F_2 depend on the number of traits you are selecting for and on the number and nature of the genes involved—that is, whether they are dominant, recessive, or additive. Additive genes are those that are neither dominant or recessive; their expression is dose dependent. (For details on segregation of genes and on selection, consult a basic genetic or breeding text, such as *The Genetics of Garden Plants* by M. B. Crane and W. J. C. Lawrence, Macmillan Co., London, 1952; or *General Genetics*, a college level text, by A. M. Srb et al., W. H. Freeman and Co., San Francisco, 1965.)

Since the effectiveness of selection decreases as the number of traits increases, we can express this relationship mathematically. If n traits are selected for, the effectiveness of selection for any one alone drops to $\sqrt[n]{v}$, where v is the size of the population from which one is selecting. Stated another way, the same degree of selection is exerted for one trait in a population of ten as in a population of 10,000, if in the latter case four traits are selected for simultaneously.

If the desired recombinant does not appear in the F_2, and if it seems that a large number of plants will have to be grown to make it appear, then grow third- and fourth-generation seedlings instead of more F_2's. Thus, if we are selecting for a mountain laurel recombinant which will be dwarf, red-bud, and feather-petaled, it may not be practical to grow enough F_2 seedlings to recombine all three traits. An F_2 which is, say, dwarf and red-bud could be crossed with one that was dwarf and feather-petaled. By crossing two of the best F_2 seedlings that express separately all the desired traits, the odds of recovering the desired recombination in the F_3 is increased. By going to the F_3 and successive generations, fewer plants need to be grown, but more time is needed to grow the successive generation.

BACKCROSS

The term backcross is applied to crossing an F_1 hybrid with one of the original parents. The backcross can be used to maintain the identity of one parent (species) and to incorporate a particular trait from a second parent (species). The fastest way to do this is to cross the first generation hybrid back to the parent with the most desirable trait. Two or more generations of backcrossing may be necessary, but this is practical only if the characteristic being incorporated shows some dominance in the F_1.

If you want to produce a plant with the small size and rooting ease of sandhill laurel but one which still resembles mountain laurel, then backcross the F_1 hybrid to mountain laurel (possible, of course, only if the F_1 is fertile).

CHROMOSOMES

Strand-like structures called *chromosomes* are present in all living cells and contain within themselves the hereditary determinants called *genes*. Chromosomes are visible through a high-powered microscope and are most easily seen in properly stained dividing cells (Figure 10–4). The number of chromosomes in a plant cell is

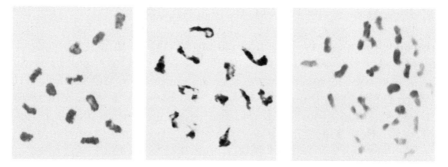

Figure 10–4   Chromosomes of three laurel species, as seen under the microscope, at the time the pollen mother cells are undergoing the reduction division, which gives each gamete half the number of chromosomes contained in other cells. Fusion of the gametes at fertilization restores the $2n$ number. The cells were stained with acetocarmine. *Left to right, Kalmia hirsuta* ($n = 12$), *K. microphylla* ($n = 12$), and *K. polifolia* ($n = 24$).

constant and usually the same for all plants in one species. Thus for any plant all the cells of the cambium, stems, roots, and leaves (somatic tissue) will have the same number of chromosomes. The chromosomes of each cell can be matched into pairs by size and shape, and if their origin could be traced, we would find that one chromosome of each pair was derived from the pollen parent and the other from the seed parent.

The number of chromosomes in a gamete (sex cell of pollen and ovary) is half the somatic number. A single set of chromosomes is referred to as the haploid number. The normal somatic number of two sets is called diploid; if four sets are present it is tetraploid. The somatic chromosome number found in the laurel species is as follows:

Species	Chromosome number
K. microphylla	24
K. polifolia	48
K. latifolia	24
K. angustifolia	24
K. cuneata	24
K. hirsuta	24
K. ericoides	unknown

We have taken up the subject of chromosome number and chromosome structure because this information is useful in planning and predicting the results of breeding experiments. In addition, unusual results from crosses can sometimes be explained by investigating chromosome number and behavior. Unfortunately, gaining this knowledge is not easy; the chromosomes of most woody plants are small, about 1/10,000 inch long. As a result, chromosome study of the laurels and their relatives has been small when compared with the many herbaceous plants and even some insects, which have considerably larger chromosomes.

POLYPLOIDS

A polyploid is an individual with more than one set of chromosomes. The eastern bog laurel with forty-eight instead of twenty-four chromosomes is a natural polyploid. Polyploid species result from a doubling of the chromosome number of an existing species, or from the hybridization of two species, and then chromosome doubling.

Triploid and tetraploid plants (one and two extra chromosome sets, respectively) are valued for their large, heavy leaves and their flowers, which often have more body and are longer lasting. Their greatest value, however, is as breeding stock.

Artificial Production of Polyploids

The chromosome number of plants can be artificially doubled through the use of colchicine. This substance affects spindle formation in dividing cells so that the chromosomes, but not the cells, divide. Application of a 0.5 to 1% concentration for eight to twenty-four hours to the shoot of a germinating seed or a developing bud results in a doubling of the chromosomes and the production of a tetraploid.

In the numerous papers on the use of colchicine by plant breeders, ericaceous plants have received little attention. But recently August Kehr of the USDA has reported successfully doubling chromosomes of azalea. Others have used colchicine successfully on blueberries.

I have treated seedlings and buds and produced polyploids of mountain laurel and sheep laurel. The most successful technique is to take newly germinated seedlings picked as soon as the cotyledons (seed leaves) spread and invert them on filter paper saturated with a 1.0% solution of colchicine in a small covered dish for eight to twenty-four hours. This technique exposes only the developing shoot to the chemical and leaves the more sensitive roots unaffected.

Artificially produced tetraploids, if fertile, can be crossed with the natural tetraploid bog laurel to produce new fertile species of hybrid original. Attempts to double the chromosome number of developing buds on F_1 hybrids of mountain laurel and sandhill laurel to restore fertility have been unsuccessful. The attempt was made by immersing a growing shoot for eight hours in a 1.0% solution of colchicine. Seedlings were not used in this case because of the difficulty in obtaining interspecific hybrid seedlings, and because they are often weak and would have difficulty surviving the treatment. When tetraploid plants of both species are available, the cross should be repeated. Seedlings from such a cross should be tetraploid and fertile. If fertile tetraploids were available of all the species, it would be worth repeating all the interspecific crosses.

RADIATION AND OTHER MUTAGENS

The use of radiation and, more recently, particular chemicals to cause the sudden genetic change known as mutation has caught the imagination of both amateur and professional plant breeders. Unfortunately, more than 99 percent of the mutations so induced are of no value. This is because a low rate of mutation occurs under natural conditions, and most of the beneficial mutations, such as those leading to increased vigor and seed production, have been selected for and incorporated into the native species. Mutation breeding has produced useful selections with grain crops, where millions of individuals can be screened in a single mutation experiment.

No doubt mutation breeding could play an important role in developing improved laurels. At present, however, breeders have so much variation available that there is little need to become deeply involved with the technique.

OBJECTIVES

The plant breeder should have definite attainable objectives. It is a waste of effort to make unplanned crosses of whatever happens to be in bloom. Acquiring the knowledge to make intelligent planning possible is half the fun of plant breeding.

The amateur plant breeder should begin with a small-scale program or he may be overwhelmed and lose his interest. The project can be expanded as interest, experience, and resources develop.

You may seek improvement in one or more of the following: (1) flowering characteristics—color, size, shape, abundance and pigment pattern; (2) seed capsule appearance and retention (fertility); (3) foliage characteristics—size, shape, color, and retention; (4) shrub form and size; (5) ease of rooting cuttings; (6) hardiness, including ability to withstand neglect and rough handling; and (7) disease and insect resistance. In setting objectives, remember that the more traits selected for at one time, the less your chances are of recovering the desired recombination among the offspring. The next two chapters review the crosses among and within species, indicating what has been done, and, perhaps more important, suggest areas for additional work.

For more on the principles of plant breeding and genetics a booklet such as the handbook *Breeding Plants for Home and Garden*, published by the Brooklyn Botanic Garden, Brooklyn, New York, 1974, is suggested.

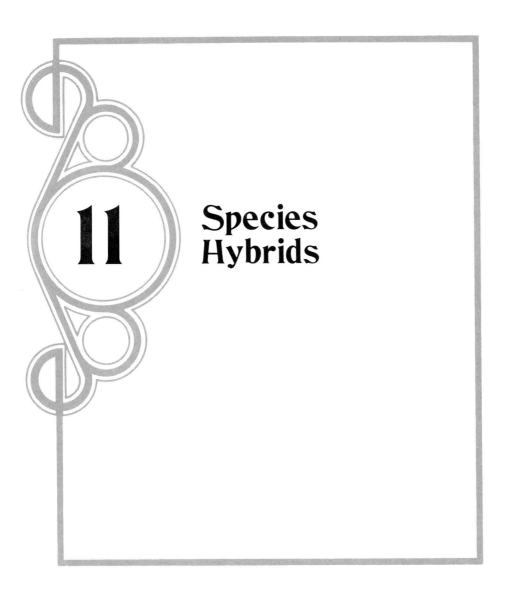

11

Species Hybrids

One of the most fascinating aspects of breeding is the potential for making hybrids between species of the same genus. There are barriers to such crosses, but the occasional successes make the attempts well worthwhile. The variation within each of the seven *Kalmia* species is considerable but could be greatly increased through interspecific crosses. By appropriate crosses of mountain laurel with the other species we could, in theory, produce mountain-laurel-like plants with deep-colored flowers, compact growth, and

135

cuttings that root readily, for these traits are available in the other species.

Six of the laurel species were crossed in all possible combinations, including reciprocals. For each species combination, at least two plants of each species and a minimum of twenty flowers were used. The average number of flowers pollinated for each of the thirty species combinations was 200. For one of the most difficult and yet occasionally successful combinations—*K. angustifolia* × *K. latifolia* —more than 1300 flowers were emasculated and pollinated, involving over twenty different plants of each species. In using different plants of a species, individuals were chosen that differed in flower

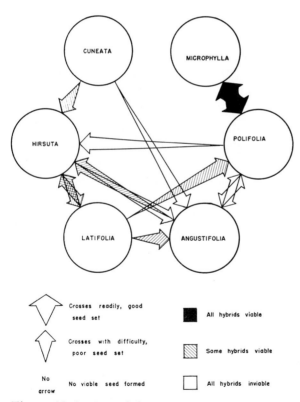

Figure 11–1   Crossibility of six laurel species for all possible F_1 combinations. (Jaynes 1968a)

color, growth habit, and geographic origin, so that failure or success would not be dependent on idiosyncrasies peculiar to a single plant.

Unfortunately, only a few of the crosses produced hybrid plants, and only the crosses between the two bog laurel species were easy to complete. The relative success of the F_1 crosses is summarized in Figure 11–1. The success rate from the crosses between species was extremely low. The amount of seed set and survival of seedlings averaged less than 1 percent of that obtained from crosses within species.

Following are some observations on the F_1 hybrids which survived more than one year. The female parent is listed first. Only three of these combinations have any ornamental or horticultural value. The least valuable ones are discussed first:

K. hirsuta × K. angustifolia

Eight hundred hybrid seeds produced only eighteen seedlings; all except four of these were weak, yellow-green plants which died within one year. *K. hirsuta* has alternately arranged leaves, while *K. angustifolia* has leaves in whorls of three. In the hybrids, whorled and alternate leaves sometimes occur on the same plant (Figure 11–2). The reciprocal cross produced no viable seedlings.

K. hirsuta × K. cuneata

Most of the seedlings produced from this cross were weak and produced at least sectors of albino or yellow-green tissue. One plant did flower but was leggy and had no particular merit as a garden plant.

K. polifolia × K. angustifolia

Only one of seventeen combinations of plants produced viable seedlings; these were weak and yellow-green, and all died within three years. In the reciprocal cross, pollen tube growth was abnormal in the style (Figure 11–3), resulting in little seed and no viable seedlings.

Figure 11–2 F₁ hybrid of *Kalmia hirsuta* and
K. angustifolia, sandhill laurel × mountain laurel, with
characters intermediate to those of the parental species. The
open flowers are just over ½ inch in diameter.

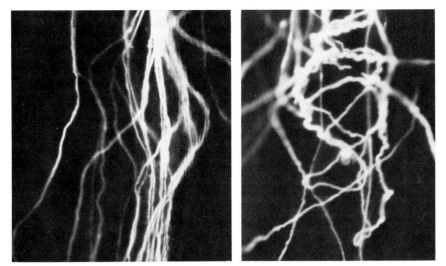

Figure 11–3   Pollen tubes growing down a style; stained with a fluorescing dye, pressed on a glass slide, and photographed through a microscope. *Left*, normal pollen tubes from a cross of sheep laurel × sheep laurel; *right*, the same seed parent, but pollen from eastern bog laurel, displaying inhibited, abnormal tube growth. Poor pollen tube growth is one reason why some of the interspecific crosses cannot be made.

K. polifolia × K. latifolia

About 4 percent of the 3000 seeds planted germinated. The seedlings were extremely variable, ranging from weak and miniature to vigorous, large plants (Figure 11–4). The hybrids resemble the female more than the male parent, but this was expected. Eastern bog laurel, as mentioned before, is a natural tetraploid with forty-eight chromosomes. Thus, *K. polifolia* contributes two sets of chromosomes to the hybrid, while mountain laurel contributes one set. The hybrid should, therefore, be a triploid with thirty-six chromosomes. This has not been confirmed, but the hybrids are pollen and seed sterile. To obtain more vigorous and possibly fertile hybrids the cross should be repeated using a tetraploid mountain laurel. (Tetraploid *K. latifolia* plants have not been verified, but a few selections, such as 'Silver Dollar', with heavy broad leaves are likely candidates.) The reciprocal cross, *K. latifolia* × *K. polifolia*,

Figure 11–4   F₁ hybrid of *K. polifolia* × *K. latifolia,* eastern bog laurel × mountain laurel. The variable seedlings are generally slow-growing and resemble their bog laurel parent. Plant on left is about 1 inch high.

results in no seed set, apparently due to an inability of the pollen of *K. polifolia* to grow down the style of *K. latifolia.*

K. latifolia × *K. hirsuta*

The only apparent difference in the reciprocal hybrid is that the seed of *K. hirsuta* can be difficult to germinate; hence, it is more convenient to use *K. latifolia* as the seed parent. The more than 200 hybrid seedlings produced from this cross were highly variable in vigor, habit, leaf shape, and flower color (Figure 11–5). Plants with leaves sectored green and white, or yellow (chlorophyll deficiencies), are common.

The hybrids are not as hardy as mountain laurel, but they will survive as far north as Connecticut. Sandhill laurel is not reliably hardy in Connecticut. Cuttings of the hybrid root more readily than those of mountain laurel. The more compact, multibranched clones

Figure 11–5 The F₁ hybrid of *K. latifolia* × *K. hirsuta*, mountain laurel × sandhill laurel. (A) The flowers are generally borne in small terminal clusters but may also occur along the stem. The leaves are about 1 inch long, or twice the length of the sandhill parent. (B) Six-month-old seedlings: mountain laurel (*left*), sandhill laurel (*right*), and two hybrids in between.

Louise Estes

Kalmia latifolia X K. hirsuta

Figure 11–6   Mountain laurel × sandhill laurel hybrid, from a watercolor
by Louise Estes of Mobile, Alabama.

have horticultural promise and are being tested for naming. Tom
Dodd Nurseries in Semmes, Alabama, has been growing these
hybrids since 1966 and plans to release five selections (Figure 11–6).

K. angustifolia × *K. latifolia*

Of the more than 2,000 seedlings germinated from nearly 10,000
seeds sown, most were yellow green and weak and eventually died.

However, when the *K. angustifolia* parent was the pure white flowering form called *candida,* the cross produced more seeds per pollinated flower, and many of the seedlings survived. The hybrids are intermediate in appearance (Figure 11–7); however, they are somewhat more tender than either parent and are slow to produce flowers. They root more readily than *K. latifolia,* and their ornamental value and hardiness in the garden are being tested. Interestingly, the reciprocal cross fails completely. Microscopic studies utilizing fluorescent stain show that the tubes from pollen of *K. angustifolia* fail to grow down the styles of *K. latifolia.*

K. polifolia × *K. microphylla* and the Reciprocal

This is the only species cross which is easy to make and consistently gives healthy, green seedlings (Figure 11–8). Because the chromosome numbers of the two are different (somatic numbers of 48 and 24, respectively) the hybrids are triploids and are generally sterile. Some of these hybrids have horticultural merit; one currently under test is named 'Rocky Top' (test number x356h). Their value rests on the fact that they are much more tolerant of the hot summers and open (snowless) winters of the northeastern United States than the western *K. microphylla,* and that they have a more compact habit than the eastern *K. polifolia.* Unfortunately, rabbits find the hybrid shoots tasty: They also enjoy the parental species. The rabbits' fondness for bog laurel is nothing new. In 1882, an anonymous writer (Alpha) reported in an English horticultural magazine that "... rabbits are very fond of it and will crop it close to the ground." The toxic effects on rabbits are not known. Another pest of the hybrid is red mites, but these are readily controlled.

The Cuban *Kalmia ericoides* is the only species that has not been crossed with the other species. Morphologically it is closely related to the sandhill laurel. Hence it may cross with *K. hirsuta,* but I would not expect it to hybridize with *K. latifolia,* a species that does cross with *K. hirsuta.* There is, however, only one way to find out, and that requires live, flowering plants or at least pollen to make the cross-pollinations.

These attempts to hybridize the species show conclusively that

Figure 11–7 The hybrid of *K. angustifolia* × *K. latifolia*, sheep laurel × mountain laurel. (A) The foliage and plant habit display many of the best characteristics of both parents; however, they are not strong growers. New growth is pale yellow-green and often tinged with pink. As the leaves mature they turn green. (B) The flowers are light pink to near white in color. Plants are slow to come into flower.

Figure 11–8   The F₁ hybrid of *K. polifolia* and *K. microphylla* var. *microphylla*, eastern bog laurel and western alpine laurel. The hybrid has many good attributes of both parents but, like them, can be difficult to keep growing well.

genetic barriers to gene flow between *Kalmia* species are well developed. Natural hybrids among the species have not been reported and the results of experimental crosses suggest that such hybrids are unlikely ever to be found. Then genetic barriers between species limit the prospects of fully utilizing the variation found among the species.

A few of the F₁ hybrids do have horticultural merit. Yet all the hybrids that have flowered are pollen and seed sterile, except for a few of the western laurel and eastern bog laurel hybrids in which only partial seed and pollen fertility was observed on only a few plants. Fertility of the F₁ hybrids might be restored by doubling the chromosome number with colchicine (see page 132). To date our limited attempts with colchicine on the hybrids have not been successful. Because of sterility problems, development of improved laurel cultivars must rely more heavily on variation within species than on variation between species.

INTERGENERIC CROSSES

Based on these observations with crosses between laurel species, we assumed that crosses at the next level, between genera, would be impossible. Well, almost! My own attempts to cross *Rhododendron* species or *Kalmiopsis leachiana* with several of the kalmias have been unsuccessful. Yet a plant does exist at the National Arboretum that may be a natural hybrid between *Rhododendron maximum* (rosebay) and mountain laurel. It is indeed an unusual plant but most likely is only an aberrant form of *R. maximum.* The leaves and flowers seem to indicate little mountain laurel parentage. A chromosome count would shed some light on the matter, because mountain laurel has twenty-four somatic chromosomes and rosebay twenty-six. An F_1 hybrid between the two would be expected to have twenty-five. The chromosomes of this putative hybrid have yet to be examined, because of the technical difficulty in preparing adequate slides for counting.

The late Halfdan Lem of Seattle, Washington, made the one apparently successful intergeneric cross between *Kalmia latifolia* (seed parent) and *Rhododendron williamsonianum* (Figure 11–9).

Figure 11–9   A hybrid of *K. latifolia* and *Rhododendron williamsonianum.*

This cross came to the attention of horticulturists when a color photograph of the plant appeared in the January, 1974, *Quarterly Bulletin* of the America Rhododendron Society. The plant gives evidence of being truly the child of the two parental species belonging to different genera. This cross is the only known exception in the laurels to the general rule that crosses do not succeed between plant genera.

The science of genetics and plant systematics helps to predict the success or failure of a cross, but the science is not developed to the point where it can predict the exceptional, successful intergeneric cross such as that performed by Lem. The usual failure of wide crosses is reason enough not to devote all one's effort to them, although the occasional and unexpected success may tempt even the conservative breeder to try a few.

Techniques of Making Controlled Crosses

12

Crosses between plants of mountain laurel are not difficult to make because the flowers are relatively large; however, dexterity is needed in handling the small flowers of sheep laurel. Controlled crosses are pointless unless there is the intention of planting the seed and nurturing the seedlings until they flower. Occasionally, desired characteristics can be determined in the seedling stage, and then only such selected seedlings need be grown. The advantage of select-

149

ing both the seed and the pollen parents lies in the tremendous increase in the odds of recovering desired types in the offspring and in the ability to repeat the cross exactly.

The principles of the crossing technique are simple. Before the flowers open, remove the male parts. When the stigma becomes receptive, apply pollen from the male parent. If the cross is successful, the resulting seed will produce hybrid seedlings. Crosses can be made in a greenhouse, outdoors, or even between distant plants. Geographically distant plants, as well as plants which flower at different times, can be cross-bred by the techniques of storing and shipping pollen.

ISOLATION BY EMASCULATION

Flowers to be used as females should be selected before they have opened. Otherwise there is no way to tell if they are pollinated or not. Use the largest tight buds. Small buds fail to develop after emasculation. To emasculate use tweezers (forceps) to remove the corolla and the ten anthers (Figure 12–1). In this way, not only are the anther sacs and pollen removed to prevent self-pollination, but by removing the corolla you remove the visual attractant and landing platform for insects. Remove all flower buds within 1 foot of the emasculated ones to prevent insect activity in the area and thereby reduce chances for contamination of the emasculated flowers.

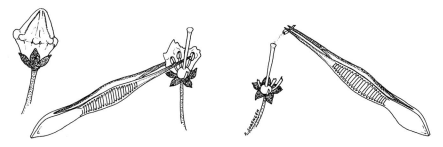

Figure 12–1   Steps in the process of emasculation and pollination. *Left*, flower bud at proper stage for emasculation. *Center*, removal of the anthers and corolla. *Right*, pollination, usually carried out a day after emasculation.

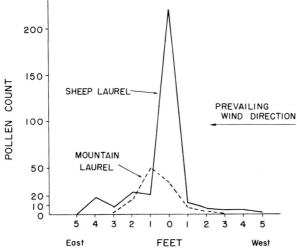

Figure 12–2 Distribution of airborne pollen
from mountain laurel and sheep laurel, caught on
petroleum-jelly-coated slides and counted after
twenty-four hours of exposure. The results
support other evidence that the pollen is not
primarily airborne. Of the two species used here,
one, sheep laurel, has pollen which is loose and
free as it comes from the anther, whereas pollen
of mountain laurel clings together.

As described in Chapter 2 the laurels are insect-pollinated. Because of the spring-loaded anthers, and the powdery pollen of some
of the species, we were curious about airborne pollen distribution.
So we placed glass slides greased with Vaseline on stakes 1 foot high
and 1 foot apart in a line from east to west among flowering sheep
laurel and in another test among mountain laurel. The results are
shown in Figure 12–2. Pollen blew downwind, but most of it fell
within 2 feet of the plant. These experiments demonstrated that
pollen can in fact be airborne for short distances but that it is not
widely distributed in air. The hybridizer should take heed. When
using large plants for crosses, and when it is impractical to remove
all the flowers, use flowers near the top to lessen the chance of pollen
contamination from above. These simple precautions make bagging
unnecessary and accidental outcrossing rare.

POLLINATION

Although the stigma may be receptive at the time of emasculation, wait and apply the pollen the next day. The stigma is receptive if it is viscid and moist. The pollen of mountain laurel and sandhill laurel clump together. With these species the whole anther can be transferred to the stigma. There it can be gently tapped or teased with the forceps to release pollen onto the stigmatic surface. If you place the pore end of the anther against the stigma, the sticky surface will catch a mass of pollen from the anther. This method works with sheep laurel and white wicky, but their pollen readily scatters. To avoid difficulty, collect anthers from about-to-open or newly opened flowers where the anthers are still held in the anther pockets. To remove the anther without losing the pollen pinch the filament with tweezers just below the anther sacs and place the anther along with others in a vial. The pollen will collect on the bottom of the vial and can be picked up on a slightly moistened artist's brush and applied to the stigmas.

POLLEN STORAGE

Pollen will remain viable for at least a week when stored at normal room temperature and humidity and out of direct sunlight. To ship pollen, place the anthers removed from the flowers in gelatin capsules (available from druggists). To guard against high humidity and mold during shipment, put the capsules in a larger container with a drying agent such as silica gel or calcium chloride.

Long-term storage is possible by drying and refrigerating the pollen. Do this by placing the pollen in a small open vial or in a gelatin capsule which is placed inside a larger closed vial containing a drying agent. Label the container clearly with type pollen and date collected. In four to eight hours when the pollen has dried, place the closed vial in a freezer (0 to $-20°F$). Laurel pollen stored in this manner for a year has been used successfully in crosses. This storage method is valuable when the flowering times of the parent plants are different.

CAGING (A LAZY MAN'S WAY TO PRODUCE HYBRID SEED)

Emasculation and pollination of individual flowers are tedious tasks, especially if large quantities of seed are desired from the crosses. Results from hand pollination of mountain laurel and sheep laurel showed that seed set from cross-pollination is 85 percent more successful than seed set from self-pollination. This led us to experiment with two plants of the same species in a cage with bumblebees. The scheme has worked, selfing is minimal, and hybrid seed is produced in quantity.

The cages were made of cube-shaped wooden frames covered on five sides with aluminum screening (Figure 12–3). The plants were planted next to each other in the spring, and, just before the flowers opened, the cage was placed over them and sealed around the lower edge with two inches of soil. When the flowers began to open on both plants, a bumblebee was released under one edge by temporarily removing some soil with a trowel.

Catching the bees was a challenge. Our first attempts with nets were hazardous at best. To reach black locust flowers, where bees were plentiful, we would drive under a tree and, standing on the

Figure 12–3   Controlled cross-pollination with bees. Parent plants are set close together and covered with a screened cage prior to flowering. Cage excludes pollinating insects, except for one or two bees introduced at onset of flowering to effect cross-pollination. True-breeding, red-budded mountain laurel seed has been produced in such cages.

van's roof, operate a long-handled insect net. Securing a bee in the net was only half the problem; getting it into a jar proved fully as risky! The adversity, however, soon led to devising a better technique. The net was discarded and the bees were collected directly in quart jars from a variety of flowers. They were easiest to catch from shrubs with deep-throated flowers, like weigelia, where our approach could be made while the bee remained busy within the flower.

In the first caging experiments we even washed the bees in lukewarm water to remove pollen on the chance that they might be carrying laurel pollen. Bathing a bee sounds tricky but was accomplished simply by placing two jars together, the lower with the water and the upper with the bee. A flat cardboard lid on the jar with the bee was slid from between the two jars and the bee landed in the water. After a quick rinse, the water was drained and the wet and befuddled bee taken to the caged plants. In subsequent experiments we decided that the washing was unnecessary as long as the bees were collected several hundred feet from flowering laurel.

The cages were checked every day or two. If the bee had died, a fresh one was put in. After all the laurel flowers had faded the cages were removed.

The amount of seed obtained depends on the number of flowers, the cross involved, and weather. For example, the 1972 flowering season in Connecticut was so wet that many flowers collapsed (molded) without setting any seed. A few of the plants, including some of the highly selected red-buds, have shown partial pollen sterility and low seed set. To maximize seed set from controlled crosses, avoid such infertile plants, and, if possible, cage several plants together to increase cross-fertilization and seed set.

Be careful with insecticides when bees are used. If you must combat leaf rollers or other insects on the caged laurel, spray them several days before the plants flower with a short residual spray (like pyrethrin), or delay the spraying until after flowering.

Honeybees are neither effective pollinators of laurel flowers nor do they survive for more than a day away from the hive. Bumblebees can, however, survive in the cages, if enough flowers are open to provide nectar and pollen for the entire flowering period of two weeks. I have used cages successfully to obtain seeds for red-budded and white-flowered mountain laurel and for white-flowered sheep laurel. With the proper inheritance information, true-breeding seed of other types of laurel could also be produced by the same method. The bee cages worked even with the interspecific cross of sheep laurel by mountain laurel. We estimated that one cage over a sheep laurel and a mountain laurel plant saved us the two to three man-days which would have been needed to emasculate the more than 1500 flowers by hand. In addition, the rate of seed set was probably higher from the bees than we could have gotten from hand emasculation and pollination. Bumblebees are more successful because of their light touch and the fact that they visit each flower many times.

There is no reason why bumblebees could not be used advantageously in making controlled crosses of other ornamentals, such as azaleas and rhododendrons, especially where large quantities of hybrid seed are desired. Ultimately propagation of selected forms will be accomplished by the rooting of cuttings from named cultivars, but in the meantime bee cages can be used to obtain large quantities of seed of known parentage.

Inheritance of Flower Color and Other Selected Traits

13

It takes a long time to accumulate data on the inheritance of specific traits. Despite the more than 1200 controlled crosses made between and within laurel species since 1961 at the Connecticut Agricultural Experiment Station, reliable inheritance data are available for only a relatively few traits. Most is known about the more unusual kinds of mountain laurel.

At least twenty-five major flower and foliage traits of mountain laurel have been identified (Table 13–1). Of these, inheritance data

Table 13–1 Existing variations of mountain laurel and representative named cultivars.*

Flower types
  Bud color
    white ('Stillwood')
    pink ('Clementine Churchill')
    red ('Ostbo Red')
  Corolla, inside ground color
    white ('Stillwood')
    pink ('Brilliant')
    candy stripe
  Pigment distribution on inside of corolla
    (A) no spots at anther pockets
        spots at anther pockets ('Splendens')
        interrupted band (*fuscata* types)
        continuous band (*fuscata* types)
        broad, continuous band virtually filling corolla (*fuscata* types, 'Goodrich')
    (B) no pigmented circle at base of corolla
        heavily pigmented circle at base of corolla
        heavily pigmented circle with five radiating points (star-ring)
  Corolla shape
    normal with five rounded to pointed lobes
    multilobed, up to nine lobes instead of five (expression often variable)
    five deeply cut lobes that reflex ('Shooting Star')

* Considerable variation exists within some of these arbitrarily designated types. This list neither classifies nor indicates many of the subtle variations that exist to distinguish among those plants which appear superficially to be similar.

lobes completely cut, five petals usually strap-like (*poly-petala* forms)
    reduced corolla ('Bettina')
    no corolla (*apetala*)
  Flower size
    normal
    large ('Silver Dollar')
  Flower distribution
    loose inflorescences
    tight ball-shaped inflorescences
  Time of flowering
    normal
    early
    late ('Shooting Star')
Foliage and plant habit
  Growth habit
    normal
    compact
    miniature (*myrtifolia* forms)
  Leaf shape
    normal
    willow-leaved ('Willowcrest')
    ovate
    large ('Silver Dollar')
  Leaf color
    all green
    sectored, white and green, and sometimes yellow-green

are available for about ten. The extent of natural variation is less well known in the other species, and, of course, there is a corresponding lack of information on the inheritance of unusual traits in these other species.

MOUNTAIN LAUREL

Little plant selection or breeding to date has been designed to extend the length of the flowering season. Variations occur in mountain laurel, but the normal flowering season lasts about three weeks. Having some plants that flower a week earlier and others two weeks later could effectively double the length of the blooming season.

The age at which seedlings flower varies from plant to plant as does the abundance of the flowers. Such variation occurs among different mountain laurel crosses and sister seedlings as well. The most precocious seedlings are often those that continue to produce flowers in successive years. Thus, breeding plants that flower at a young age and that flower profusely each year should not be difficult.

White Bud and Corolla Color

A pure white (one lacking the red pigment anthocyanin) has not yet been verified. Crosses among plants with nearly pure white flowers will produce all light-colored or white-flowered plants. Crosses of deep pink and white result in seedlings with a variable, intermediate pink color range. The purer the white parent, the less likely is pink to be strongly expressed in the offspring. Seedlings of 'Stillwood', a good white (Color Plate Figure 3), seldom have much pink color even when the other parent is a strong pink, because white is dominant to red bud color.

Pink Bud and Corolla Color

Numerous shades and patterns of pink exist, and crosses of pink parents generally produce a range of pink types. The results of crosses among the deepest pinks suggest that a true-breeding line can be developed. Apparently several major and modifying genes affect the expression of pink flower color. One of our best crosses between two deep pink plants gave us seedlings, all with richly colored flowers; of thirty-five seedlings, thirty flowered in the fourth growing season, fully a year earlier than the seedlings of many other crosses.

Among the crosses of deep pink and red-budded plants, a low frequency of dwarf seedlings with purplish foliage may appear. Although the seedlings are vigorous at first, we have been unsuccessful in raising them to maturity.

Red Bud Color

Although no mountain laurel with a solid red corolla is known, plants with brilliant red buds can be bred true from seed (Color Plate Figure 11). These red-buds are often almost iridescent and some so intensely pigmented that they have a purplish black hue. However, only plants grown in sunlight attain full expression of this trait. It is recessive to white and the normal flower bud color, but pigmentation on the inside of the corolla is under separate genetic control and may be white or pink in color. Because the red bud character is recessive, plants breed true when intercrossed and can be mass-produced from seed using caged bees as described in Chapter 12. Lack of vigor noted in some of these red-bud crosses may be due to inbreeding that inadvertently resulted from the intense selection practiced in developing these vibrantly colored plants.

As indicated, red-bud seedlings are distinctive as a class yet variable among themselves. Plants with lighter colored red buds may be difficult to distinguish from those with deep pink buds. 'Ostbo Red' selected in cultivation on the West Coast was the first red-bud clone named and vegetatively propagated.

Banded (*fuscata*)

The banded laurels form a distinct class, but considerable variation exists in the width, pigmentation, and continuity of their band. Presence of the band itself is controlled by a single dominant gene (*B*); other genes cause size and color modification. One unusual plant was discovered in our plantings in 1973. All the flowers on the plant were characterized by a narrow band except for one cluster on one branch which had flowers with an intense broad band (Figure 13–1). Crosses using the two kinds of flowers on this plant

Figure 13–1   Banded mountain laurel with a broad deeply colored ring, found in the same native population of laurel as "Goodrich" (see Plate 7). The trait is apparently controlled by a single dominant gene, as in other banded types.

may shed light on the genetic differences between narrow- and broad-banded plants. Possibly the extremely broad-banded types are the double dominant (*BB*), but this is not apparent in the segregated F_2's observed. So far, all banded plants when crossed with the normal have produced plants with banding among half of them. We are searching for a plant carrying both dominant genes for banding. Seedlings of such a homozygous or double dominant would all be banded regardless of the pollen parent.

Star-Ring

This characteristic was first observed by Edmund Mezitt in one of his plants at Weston Nurseries in Massachusetts in 1968. It is distinguished from the normal type by the greater prominence of the inner pigmented ring and especially by the five radiating points which travel up the creases of the corolla to the margin of the flower (Color Plate Figure 4). Star-ring was crossed with three other plants having prominent but not starred rings. Of forty-five flowering seedlings, just over one-half had the star-ring trait. Thus the star-ring appears to be under the control of a single dominant gene (*Sr*).

A striking ornamental selection would result if the pigmentation and width of this star pattern could be enhanced. To obtain such a plant I have intercrossed star-ring plants to obtain the homozygous dominant; in addition, F_2 crosses were made of star-ring with plants having unusually broad rings. The seedlings have not yet flowered.

Stem and Foliage Color

White flowered plants have green stems and leaves whereas deep pink and red flowered plants often, but not always, have purplish-red stems and reddish-bronze new foliage. The inheritance of these attractive color traits of stem and foliage has not been worked out.

Feather-Petal (*polypetala*)

This form with strap-like petals was first described in 1871 in Massachusetts. Analysis of several first- and second-generation crosses indicates that the character is controlled by a single recessive gene (*P*). A great deal of variation exists in expression of the trait from partially to fully cut corollas (Figure 13–2). The relationship of the feather-petal sort to corolla types like 'Shooting Star' and 'Bettina' has not been established, but preliminary results indicate they are under the control of different genes.

Apetala

Plants of this form lack a corolla, but they have functional anthers and pistils (Figure 13–2). Like *polypetala*, *apetala* is apparently under the control of a single recessive gene. When crossed with normal mountain laurel, all the offspring are normal; but when these F_1's are backcrossed to the *apetala* parent the seedlings segregate, with one-half being apetalous.

Figure 13–2   A collection of unusual mountain laurel flowers from different plants. (A) Three different expressions of the feather-petal (*apetala*) trait. The lowest cluster is derived from a banded-feather-petal cross and expresses the banded (*fuscata*) pigmentation on the strap-like petals. (B) *Top*, 'Bettina'; *middle*, an unnamed clone; *bottom, apetala*. (C) *Top*, a larger than normal flower with six, instead of the normal five, lobes; *middle*, normal flower; *bottom*, an abnormal type occasionally obtained from crosses of deep-pink-colored plants.

Miniature (*myrtifolia*)

This form is in all respects a true miniature with leaves, flowers, and internodes (distance between leaves) all one-third to one-half normal size. In cultivation in Europe since 1840, it is extremely rare in the wild. Plants grown from seed obtained from open-pollinated *myrtifolia* specimens are usually normal in appearance. However if these normal looking seedlings of *myrtifolia* parentage are inter-crossed, one-fourth of the seedlings will be miniature. The form is under the control of a single recessive gene (*m*); therefore, miniatures crossed with miniatures should be true breeding for this one character. Furthermore, it should be possible to develop a race of miniature laurel and incorporate into it other interesting traits such as red-budded or banded flowers. As with the banded plants, all miniatures are not identical. In fact, there is considerable variation among them for leaf shape and general form as well as for flower color and markings on the flowers.

Compact

This form is distinguished by shortened internodes and closely packed leaves. Although a sparse bloomer, it makes an attractive, compact plant (Figure 13–3). When it does bloom, the flowers are buried in the foliage. Like *myrtifolia*, the compact trait is apparently under the control of a single recessive gene.

Figure 13–3 A compact mountain laurel, characterized by slow growth and very close spacing of leaves along the branches. This plant is at least twenty years old, 2 feet high and 3 feet across. It is sparse flowering, and often the few flowers produced are buried in the foliage. Sheep laurel can be seen in the background.

Variegated Foliage

These plants have leaves and whole shoots that are sectored green and white or yellow. Several reciprocal crosses indicate that this trait is not transmitted through the pollen (male parent) but only through the egg (female parent). A factor in the cytoplasm (extra-chromosomal material) may be responsible. Other types of sector-ing and chlorophyll mottling have been observed, and certainly the different kinds may be under different sorts of genetic control. The attractive and unusual foliage color pattern give these forms good ornamental potential (Figure 13–4).

Albino Seedlings

Commonly about 1 percent albino seedlings occur among newly germinated seedlings. Lacking chlorophyll and the ability to manu-

Figure 13–4   A superb, sectored mountain laurel was collected in New York state several years ago by Ralph Smith but subsequently died, probably due to a root infection of phytophthora. Some of the seedlings from that plant have the sectored trait and may be worth propagating. Sectors on a plant may be white, yellow, or yellow-green and in various patterns. The sectoring in A is typical. The sectoring on the branch

facture food, these soon die. A much higher proportion of albino seedlings occurs among crosses of some of the banded plants. The percentage varies widely from 14 to 65 percent but is generally about 25 percent, suggesting that the cause may be a single recessive gene. The reason for the wide variation in frequency of albinos from the different crosses is not yet understood.

SHEEP LAUREL

White Flowers

Sheep laurel plants that have white flowers lack the red pigment anthocyanin. As young seedlings they can be recognized by the lack of red pigment in the stems and leaves. White-flowering sheep laurel plants are rare in the wild, but they are not difficult to reproduce from seed. The presence of color is governed by a single dominant

shown in B is atypical in that it is marginal rather than radiating from the midvein. Bassett described a similar laurel, with a white marginal variegation, in 1893, but the border was so narrow as to be judged not worth propagating. Sectored seedlings of sheep laurel are not uncommon but seldom maintain the character to maturity.

gene (A); hence, white plants are homozygous recessives (aa). When two white-flowered plants are intercrossed, all the seedlings are white-flowered. We have demonstrated that the bee-caging technique described in Chapter 12 can readily be used to mass produce seed of white-flowering sheep laurel.

One of the interesting findings in studies of the white-flowered sheep laurel was that, although white-flowered plants are seldom found in nature, the recessive gene is present in a high frequency in some populations. In a population of 300 flowering, colored plants in Madison, Connecticut, it was estimated that 24 percent carried a single recessive gene for white.

Collections and Sources of Laurel

An Abbreviated List of Gardens and Nurseries

Arnold Arboretum, Jamaica Plain,
   Massachusetts
Bartlett Arboretum of the University of
   Connecticut, Stamford, Connecticut
Calloway Gardens, Pine Mountain, Georgia
Connecticut Agricultural Experiment
   Station, New Haven, Connecticut
Tom Dodd Nurseries, Semmes, Alabama
Garden-in-the-Woods, Sudbury,
   Massachusetts
Greer Gardens Nursery, Eugene, Oregon
Henry Foundation, Gladwyne,
   Pennslyvania
Holden Arboretum, Mentor, Ohio
Kalmthout Arboretum, Kalmthout,
   Belgium
Mayfair Nurseries, Nichols, New York
North Carolina Botanical Garden,
   University of North Carolina, Chapel
   Hill, North Carolina
Royal Botanic Gardens, Edinburgh,
   Scotland

Royal Horticultural Gardens (Wisley),
Ripley, Surrey, England
Sheffield Park, Uckfield, England
Skylands of Ringwood State Park,
Ringwood, New Jersey
Susie Harwood Garden, University of
North Carolina, Charlotte, North
Carolina
United States National Arboretum,
Washington, D.C.
Weston Nurseries, Hopkinton,
Massachusetts

Bibliography

Alpha. 1882. Garden flora. *The Garden* 52:6–7.

Anonymous. 1956. Plant pest handbook. *Conn. Agr. Exp. Sta. Bull.* 600:194 pp.

Bartron, B. S. 1802. Some accounts of the poisonous and injurious honey of North America. *Trans. Amer. Philos. Soc.* 5:51–70.

Bassett, W. F. 1893. A variegated-leaved *Kalmia. Gardening* 1:222.

Beal, W. J. 1867. Agency of insects in fertilizing plants. *Amer. Nat.* 1:254–260.

Bean, W. J. 1897. Trees and shrubs. *Gardens* 52:77–78.

Benson, A. B. 1937. *Peter Kalm's travels in North America.* New York: Wilson-Erickson.

Britton, E. G. 1913. Wild plants needing protection. *Jour. New York Bot. Garden* 14:121–123.

Buttrick, P. L. 1924. Connecticut's state flower, the mountain laurel, a forest plant. Yale Univ., New Haven, Conn., *Marsh Bot. Garden Publ.* 1:1–28.

Clawson, A. B. 1933. Alpine kalmia (*Kalmia microphylla*) as a stock-poisoning plant. *U.S. Dept. Agr. Tech. Bull.* 391:1–9.

Copeland, H. F. 1943. A study, anatomical and taxonomic, of the genera of Rhododendroideae. *Amer. Midl. Nat.* 30:533–625.

Crane, M. B., and W. J. C. Lawrence. 1938. *The genetics of garden plants.* 2nd ed. London: Macmillan. 287 pp.

Crawford, A. C. 1908. Mountain laurel, a poisonous plant. *U.S. Dept. Agr. Bur. Pl. Ind. Bull.* 121:21–35.

Davis, L. D. 1957. Flowering and alternate bearing. *Proc. Amer. Soc. Hort. Sci.* 70:545–556

Ebinger, J. E. 1974. A systematic study of the genus *Kalmia* (*Erica-ceae*). Rhodora 76:315–398.

Flemer, William, III. 1949. The propagation of *Kalmia latifolia* from seed. *Bull. Torrey Bot. Club* 76:12–16.

Forbes, E. B., and S. I. Bechdel. 1930. Mountain laurel and *Rhodo-dendron* as food for the white-tailed deer. *Ecology* 12:323–333.

Gray, A. 1877. Large trunks of *Kalmia latifolia*. *Amer. Nat.* 11:175.

Hardin, J. W., and J. M. Arena. 1969. *Human poisoning from native and cultivated plants*. Durham, N.C.: Duke Univ. Press.

Heichel, G. H., and R. A. Jaynes. 1974. Stimulating emergence and growth of *Kalmia* genotypes with CO_2. *HortScience* 9:60–62.

Holmes, E. M. 1884. Medical plants used by the Cree Indians, Hudson's Bay territory. *Amer. Jour. Pharm.* 56:617–621.

Holmes, M. L. 1956. *Kalmia*, the American laurels. *Baileya* 4:89–94.

Howes, F. N. 1949. Sources of poisonous honey. *Kew Bull.* 1949: 167–171.

Jaynes, R. A. 1968a. Interspecific crosses in *Kalmia*. *Amer. Jour. Bot.* 55:1120–1125.

———. 1968b. Self incompatibility and inbreeding depression in three laurel (*Kalmia*) species. *Proc. Amer. Soc. Hort. Sci.* 93: 618–622.

———. 1968c. Breaking seed dormancy of *Kalmia hirsuta* with high temperatures. *Ecology* 49:1196–1198.

———. 1969. Chromosome counts of *Kalmia* species and revalua-tion of *K. polifolia* var. *microphylla*. *Rhodora* 71:280–284.

———. 1971a. Laurel selections from seed: true-breeding red-budded mountain laurel. *Conn. Agr. Exp. Sta. Cir.* 240, 10 pp.

———. 1971b. A gene controlling pigmentation in sheep laurel. *Jour. Hered.* 62:201–203.

———. 1971c. Seed germination of six *Kalmia* species. *Jour. Amer. Soc. Hort. Sci.* 96:668–672.

———. 1971d. The Kalmias and their hybrids. *Quart. Bull. Amer. Rhododendron Soc.* 25:160–164.

———. 1971e. The selection and propagation of improved *Kalmia latifolia* cultivars. *Proc. Int. Plant Prop. Soc.* 21:366–374.

———. 1974. Inheritance of flower and foliage characteristics in mountain laurel (*Kalmia latifolia* L.). *Jour. Amer. Soc. Hort. Sci.* 99:209–211.

Jaynes, R. A., and C. D. Clayberg (eds.). 1974. *Handbook on breed-*

ing plants for home and garden. Plants and Gardens, Brooklyn Botanic Garden, N.Y. 30:1–76.

Johnson, E. A., and J. L. Kovner. 1956. Effects on stream flow of cutting a forest understory. *Forest Sci.* 2:82–91.

Kingsbury, J. M. 1964. *Poisonous plants of the United States and Canada.* Englewood Cliffs, N.J.: Prentice-Hall.

Kurmes, E. A. 1961. The ecology of mountain laurel in southern New England, Ph.D. dissertation, Yale Univ., New Haven, Conn. 85 pp.

Leach, David G. 1961. *Rhododendrons of the world and how to grow them.* New York: Scribner. 544 pp.

Lipp, Lewis F. 1973. Propagating broad-leafed evergreens. In *Handbook on broad leaved evergreens.* Plants and Gardens, Brooklyn Botanic Garden, N.Y. 29:78–80.

Lovell, J. H., and H. B. Lovell. 1934. The pollination of *Kalmia angustifolia. Rhodora* 36:25–28.

Marsh, C. D., and A. B. Clawson. 1930. Mountain laurel (*Kalmia latifolia*) and sheep laurel (*Kalmia angustifolia*) as stock-poisoning plants. *U.S. Dept. Agr. Tech. Bull.* 219:1–22.

Mastalerz, J. W. 1968. CO_2 enrichment for a small greenhouse. *Flower and Garden.* Nov. pp. 27, 28, 47.

Muenscher, W. C. 1957. *Poisonous plants of the United States.* Rev. ed. New York: Macmillan.

Nichols, L. P. 1955. Diseases of ornamental shrubs and vines. *Penn. State Univ., Coll. Agr. Ext. Serv. Cir.* 429, 26 pp.

Nicholson, S., and J. F. Clovis. 1967. Dye plants and dye methods in West Virginia. *Castanea* 32:111–116.

Peterson, E. B. 1965. Inhibition of black spruce primary roots by a water-soluble substance in *Kalmia angustifolia. Forest Sci.* 11:473–479.

Pirone, Pascal P. 1970. *Diseases and pests of ornamental plants.* 4th ed. New York: Ronald. 546 pp.

Pritchard, W. R. 1956. Laurel (*Kalmia angustifolia*) poisoning of sheep. *N. Amer. Veterinarian* 37:461–462.

Rehder, A. 1910. Notes on the forms of *Kalmia latifolia.* Rhodora 12:1–3.

Southall, R. M., and J. W. Hardin. 1974. A taxonomic revision of *Kalmia* (Ericaceae). *Jour. Elisha Mitchell Sci. Soc.* 90:1–23.

Sprague, E. 1871. *The Rhododendron and American Plants.* Boston: Little, Brown.

Tallent, W. H., Mary L. Riethof, and E. C. Horning. 1957. Studies on the occurrence and structure of acetylandromedol (andromedotoxin). *Jour. Amer. Chem. Soc.* 79:4548–4554.

Trumpy, J. R. 1893. Propagating kalmias. *Gardening* 1:222.

Wahlenberg, W. G., and W. T. Doolittle. 1950. Reclaiming Appalachian brush lands for economic forest production. *Jour. Forestry* 48:170–174.

Waud, R. A. 1940. The action of *Kalmia angustifolia* (lambkill). *Jour. Pharm. Exp. Ther.* 69:103–111.

Wood, C. E., Jr. 1961. The genera of Ericaceae in the southeastern United States. *Jour. Arnold Arb.* 42:10–80.

Wood, H. B., V. L. Stromberg, J. C. Keresztesy, and E. C. Horning. 1954. Andromedotoxin. A potent hypotensive agent from *Rhododendron maximum. Jour. Amer. Chem. Soc.* 76:5689–5692.

Index

178